DEVELOPING A PROFESSIONAL
VITA OR RESUME

Third Edition

by Carl McDaniels

Professor of Education

Virginia Tech

with

Editorial Assistance

from

Mary Anne Knobloch

About the Author...

Carl McDaniels has worked as a teacher, career counselor, adviser, and served as a counselor educator for over 45 years. Since 1969 he has been in counselor education at Virginia Tech in Blacksburg, Virginia. And served 16 years as director for the Virginia Career Information Delivery System (Virginia VIEW). He was previously on the faculty at George Washington University and for six years was director of Processional Services for what is now the American Counseling Association (ACA).

Dr. McDaniels has served as president of the National Capital Personnel and Guidance Association, the Virginia Career Development Association (VCDA), and the National Career Development Association (NCDA). He has been a frequent consultant and workshop leader in the area of counseling and career development. He authored Finding Your First Job for Houghton-Mifflin. He wrote The Changing Workplace and Counseling for Career Development (with Norman Gysbers) for Jossey-Bass and a series of over 50 career education wall charts for Garrett Park Press.

His own work as a member of search committees and his conviction that too many applicants lost out on key positions because they did such a poor job on their professional vitae, encouraged Dr. McDaniels to conduct a series of clinics on how to prepare a vita. The response to those clinics and the current demand for this information led to the development of this book and its popularity has extended to a third edition.

About the Editorial Assistant...

Mary Anne Knobloch received her doctorate from Virginia Tech in July 1996. She had served as user service manager for the Virginia Career Information Delivery System, (Virginia VIEW) from 1990-1995. Before that she was a counselor with the Virginia Employment Commission for 16 years. During that time, she reviewed thousands of resumes and other job search correspondence. She observed that many qualified people removed themselves from serious consideration by submitting inadequate resumes including many without names, telephone numbers, or previous employer locations. Much of the job search correspondence she reviewed lacked clear focus. She was pleased to assist dr. McDaniels with this book that informs professionals on how to write winning vitae and resumes.

Library of Congress Cataloging-in-Publication Data

McDaniels, Carl.
    Developing a professional vita or resume / by Carl McDaniels. --
Rev. ed.
    p.   cm.
     ISBN 0-89434-178-2 (alk. paper)
     1. Resumes (Employment)   I. Title.
HF5383.M18   1997   97-41900
650.14--dc20   CIP

Published and Distributed by
Ferguson Publishing Company
200 West Madison, Suite 300
Chicago, IL 60606
312-580-5480

Printed in the United States of America
U-6

Table of Contents

Foreword to The Third Edition

This book has been many years in the making. Its content gradually emerged as the result of reviewing hundreds of poorly prepared professional summaries--and an occasional good one. In the early 1970s, with the encouragement of then Dean Karl T. Hereford of the College of Education at Virginia Tech, I began to hold regular seminars for faculty colleagues in vita development. Later, graduate and undergraduate students requested the same kind of help, which led to annual sessions for them. After several years, enough materials developed to convince me that there was strong content for a useful book. This publication seeks to fill the void that exists in this important area of professional development. Clearly there are dozens of resume books--both general and specific. There are now a few vita books as well. This book tries to deal with the bigger issues and general principles of developing professional summaries. This book presents the process of developing professional summaries with a few examples so that once readers, are presented with the key points and several examples, they can put together their own best vita or resume.

The purpose of this book is to help people, mainly in higher education, to prepare their best vita or resume. It does not simply present page after page of examples. It is meant to emphasize a broad set of guidelines for professionals to collect and present. This third edition emphasizes how to develop an ongoing professional portfolio including worksheets to help generate an annual update of one's professional summary.

Many students and faculty helped with the first edition. The second edition benefited from many comments that readers have shared with me. Deb Hedrick and Gale Watts of Virginia Tech were especially helpful in providing thoughtful suggestions for that revision. There have been many changes in technologies, both in computers and software, as well as a wide array of paper stock and colors since the first edition. Now it is becoming more common to send professional summaries electronically and/or having them "scanned" into a computer. This new trend may change how some resumes and vitas are transmitted, but it will not alter the principles for understanding how to collect and present information. This third edition has likewise benefited from reader comments, colleagues critiques, and the professional editorial assistance of Dr. Mary Anne Knobloch, my long-time co-worker at Virginia VIEW.

Carl McDaniels

Blacksburg, Virginia
August 1996

Chapter 1

Introduction

FACULTY OPENING- Lavier University seeks an Assistant Professor of Philosophy for a two-year position, with a possibility of contract renewal. Twelve-hour undergraduate teaching load. Ph.D. required, teaching experience desirable, but not necessary. Salary negotiable. Vacancy is for Fall term. Application deadline is April 15. Send Vita and Cover Letter to Professor Jane Doe, Lavier University, Southern, South Carolina 29666-1212.

This book has a unique focus. It is prepared for the professional who frequently needs a formal summary of education and work background. A professional vita is of prime interest to people in institutions of higher education or those in closely related settings such as publishing, research and development, government service, or professional associations. Resumes, on the other hand, are of particular interest to those seeking positions in business, social service, and related general employment. Regardless of the type of position one is seeking, a vita or resume should be viewed as a document that briefly tells people who you are. It is a document that can pave the road to simple introductions at meetings or to an interview. Viewed in this light, job seekers should look at their skills, qualifications, and accomplishments as goods, products, and services they have to offer a potential employer.

The audience for whom this book is intended is most likely to pursue job hunting on its own rather than through placement or executive search services. It is also most likely to respond to notices of vacancies listed at association conventions or in professional journals and trade publications such as The Chronicle of Higher Education, the Library Journal, Publisher's Weekly, Chemical and Engineering News, the American Counseling Association's (ACA) Counseling Today, and the Affirmative Action Register. A typical advertisement is shown above.

Too often, graduate students assume they already know how to prepare a professional summary. After reading hundreds of vitas and resumes over the last 45 years, I would say nothing could be further from the truth. What seems to happen is that well-educated individuals who think that they know what they are doing mistakenly do not seek assistance when preparing their professional summaries. A university placement director commented recently: "Graduate students need tremendous amounts of help in vita preparation. It is a crime how poorly they present their qualifications."

Without assistance, too many professional summaries prepared by recent graduates are handicapped by one or more of the following problems:

omitting whole areas of their background

presenting trivia in place of substantial information

presenting information in a confusing manner

failing to adjust content to fit a specific purpose

failing to use care in preparation and duplication

failing to update annually or use recent information

including too much unimportant organizational material

lacking in scope

failing to emphasize accomplishments

and even leaving out their own name and address entirely

BUSINESS MANAGER- Large nonprofit urban corporation seeks manager to supervise clerical, bookkeeping, and maintenance department. Responsible for purchasing, preparation and supervision of annual budget. Requires a minimum of a bachelor's degree and five years of related experience in administration. Salary open. Apply to Charles Able, Personnel Manager, XYZ Cooperation P. O. Box 1977, Metropolitan, PA 19301-1977.

This book also is written for another group: people who already have positions but now are seeking promotions or professional advancement. A sales representative may want to move into sales management. A college instructor may aspire for a tenured professorship--either at the same institution or a different one. A state employee may seek a better job with another agency or a federal bureau. In some cases, a promotion is necessary to stay at an institution under an "up" or "out" philosophy--such as advancing through faculty ranks in college teaching, gaining promotions in commissioned military ranks, or progressing through stages of the U. S. Foreign Service.

This third edition is also important for people who have been caught in downsizing, cutbacks, mergers, or buyouts, who have otherwise lost their jobs, or who fear they may. It can be helpful in going back to review skills, competencies, accomplishments, activities, and responsibilities from prior work and leisure areas to fully capture your strengths in a current vita or resume. The worksheets included in chapter 4 on "Building and Maintaining a Professional Portfolio" provide a format for collecting the date needed to develop vitae and resumes.

The quality of the vita or resume could be the difference between making a key change of employment, obtaining a promotion, or being to leave an unsatisfactory place of work. Often job changes are required for personal advancement because of the current employers' small number of top jobs or limited turnover. No matter what the reason, the professional summary plays a key role in determining whether or not a person will receive favorable consideration. The appearance of the vita or resume is just as important for a senior professional as it is for a junior person just beginning a line of work. Professionals should update their vitas or resumes every January of each year as a part of a regular review of their career development situation.

This book, then, has a goal--to increase your prospects for employment or promotion through the best possible presentation of your current and prior activities accomplishments via a quality vita or resume. No book, of course, can provide you with abilities, experiences, educational credentials, or professional activities you have not earned, but it can show how to present your current and past activities in the most favorable light. As someone has said, "The worst thing professionally is to have done nothing worth putting down on paper. The next worst thing is to have something worth putting down and expressing it so poorly that it is not understood!"

Key Definitions

Considerable confusion exists over terms describing information in professional summaries. Many different terms are frequently used and the resulting confusion suggests that a standard set of definitions would be helpful. Terms used in professional journals, job vacancy notices, or placement service bulletins include the following:

credentials or papers
transcripts (sometimes called official or personal)
professional summary
vita (sometimes called vitae or curriculum vitae)
resume (sometimes proceeded by words like brief, current, master or complete)

The following definitions are used in this book. Hopefully, this may encourage further standardization of terminology:

Credentials or papers usually refer to a set of references, transcripts, and other materials used in hiring people in education or related fields. These are normally assembled by a college placement (or career services) office or a teacher placement agency. Copies are sent to prospective employers at the request of the individual concerned or sent by the office in response to listed vacancies. Since credentials follow a fixed format set by each individual placement office they will not be discussed further here.

Transcripts are official documents reporting on the courses a student took, grades and appropriate dates, as well as titles and dates of degree(s) awarded at an educational institution. Other information, such as honors, is sometimes included. Official transcripts come only from the institution. A transcript can be sent to an individual but may then only be used as an unofficial record.

Professional summary is a term which, as used in this book, includes both the vita and resume.

Vita is a comprehensive (generally three to five pages, but could be up to ten pages) biographical statement emphasizing professional qualifications, accomplishments, and activities. Often these are specifically requested by employers such as in the ad that follows for a library administrator.

Resume[1] is an individually designed summary (usually one or two pages) of personal and educational information as well as a person's experience, qualifications, and accomplishments. A resume is intended to demonstrate fitness for a particular position or type of position. It also might be developed for general introductory purposes. A resume focuses attention on an individual's strongest qualifications. It is developed to fit a specific purpose.

Cover letter is a clearly worded one-page document to highlight the most outstanding points of a person's accompanying application, vita or resume.

How do you respond to a job notice like the one for a librarian? The usual suggestion is to send a cover letter following the key points found in chapter 8 in which you indicate you are enclosing your resume, but that you will send a more detailed vita or other back-up information such as transcripts or credentials if requested. Or, if this is a post you really want and feel qualified for, you may choose to send your vita, credentials, and transcripts.

> **Library serving a community of 1,000,000 with an annual budget of $800,000 invites applications for the position as director. The successful candidate to begin work on September 1. Qualifications: MLS (ALA) with six years of public library experience at the supervisory level where superior management has been demonstrated. Salary range $28,900-$37.500, with appointment within this range determined by successful candidate's qualifications; usual fringe benefits. Send inquiries of interest to Mr. Robert Bruce, Chairperson, Search Committee, 1 North Main Street, Eastport, IL 60099-1541.**

How This Book Will Help You

This book will help you review your personal background and emerge with the most meaningful professional summary possible. The following steps will be covered in turn:

Importance of a Professional Summary (Chapter 2)
Gathering the Facts for a Professional Summary (Chapter 3)
Building and Maintaining a Professional Portfolio (Chapter 4)

Putting the Vita Together (Chapter 5)

Revising and Finalizing the Vita (Chapter 6)

Developing the Resume (Chapter 7)

Covering Cover Letters (Chapter 8)

Producing Electronic Resumes (Chapter 9)

Final Vita/Resume Checklist (Chapter 10)

Chapter 2

Importance of the Professional Summary

> **NEWS DIRECTOR-** Station WRIX has immediate opening for a news director and announcer. Applicants should have several years of varied experience in broadcast radio news and be prepared to assume responsibility for all aspects of news department. Send letter of interest and resume with tapes as soon as possible to: WRIX-AM/FM, P. O. Box 2200 Mountain Top, WV 28640-2200.

A vita or resume represents you in a variety of ways. Make yours work to your advantage. Usually a vita or resume is the first--and too often--the only impression of you seen by a reader. Unless your professional summary communicates your qualifications and accomplishments, you will never get to the application-interview stage. Keep in mind the key difference between the application and the vita or resume. The application is the employer's form and asks for data that seems most important to the organization. The vita or resume, however, are your documents and can stress areas of your strength while minimizing areas of weakness or little experience. Individuals, literally, put their best foot forward via their professional summary.

In earlier and simpler times, informal systems created more personal introductions (sometimes called "Old Boys' Networks"). Within the limited geographic area in which most people lived and worked, they knew each other. Recently, I was asked to help a person who had worked for 25 or 30 years and had never needed a resume because he had simply moved from job to job by reputation and word of mouth. Now the nation and even the entire world are potential places of employment. A job vacancy notice, like the one for station WRIX, will probably draw dozens if not hundreds of applicants from all areas of the United States. Many people would also jump at the chance to work in England, Venezuela, or Japan. For almost any professional vacancy, the relatively large number of qualified applicants almost always dictates some type of screening procedure--eliminating most applicants prior to a personal interview. Your only hope for an interview is to provide a highly competitive professional summary to get you across that first screening hurdle.

Studies report that personnel reviewers spent one minute or less reading each resume! Impressions are quickly formed--often on the basis of the resume's appearance. In short, all professional summaries have got to make a <u>strong first impression and quickly</u>. Writers must seriously ask themselves "How can I emphasize my strongest qualifications and accomplishments and present them <u>in clear, easy-to-understand, emphatic terms</u>?"

Professional people need to have available a detailed professional summary which normally includes at least the following types of information:

complete personal contact information
educational background with dates of degrees and copies of transcripts
employment experience with dates and job titles
current and past professional affiliations and honors
publications and other creative activities
civic or service activities

This book will concentrate on the development of the vita since it is the basic document for most professional people, especially in higher education. Once the person has developed the materials and format for a vita, the shorter resume should follow easily. <u>The two types of documents obviously have many things in common with comprehensiveness vs. brevity being the central distinction.</u> The focus of this book is on the vita since there are many books, booklets, and brochures about resume preparation. It is the vita which is underdeveloped in the literature, yet it is far more important for most professional people. The vita and resume have many purposes, five of which follow.

1. : Providing Information for Professional Activities

> **EMPLOYMENT AND TRAINING PAPERS-** A national forum on "Employment and Training Utilization of the Aging" will be sponsored by the U. S. Dept. of Labor in Denver, Colorado May 8-10. Those wishing to present papers should send a one-page abstract, a detailed outline and resume by January 15 to: Employment and Training Forum on the Utilization of the Aging, U. S. Dept. of Labor, Washington, D. C. 20010. For those abstracts accepted a $750 honorarium will be paid. There will be 25 papers accepted for presentation.

A vita or resume provides a useful summary to introduce a person giving a speech or when a person is inducted into an organization or honorary group. The availability of an up-to-date vita obviously saves a great deal of preparation and may eliminate the need to fill out a special application or other form. The comprehensiveness of the vita means that this summary is already written and you have only to hand out the set of pages which may help overcome your normal sense of modesty. Most of us are reluctant to "toot our horns" and we may not mention in conversation honors or other special recognition received in the past. The fact that they are included in your vita, however, means that they will be included as a part of a total picture of your background. The professional vita is like a videotape produced over a period of years, rather than a quick snapshot.

Proposals to foundations and government agencies for grants and contracts require professional summaries of key staff as a significant part of the application material. Here, too, having this available means that it can be placed, in a matter of minutes, into the appropriate section of the proposal. The detail in a vita will help answer questions about your background asked by those reviewing you--and all of their questions can never be fully anticipated. Some will focus on your educational background and related honors and activities. Others will be concerned with what you have done, especially your involvement in projects similar in size and scope to the one for which you are applying. Still others are going to give priority to your references and what they say about you. All these things are covered by a typical vita.

Candidates for advisory boards or councils often must submit a summary of qualifications. An informative vita means a better chance for a sizable honorarium and the recognition of being selected to present a paper at an important national meeting. Since these groups and members of the committees charged with making selections have broad interests, the breadth of information in a good vita should be of special interest to them.

Publishers considering a book proposal will often base their reactions on a writer's vita. If you have a requisite educational background and work experience, they will be reassured. If you have previously published in a certain area, it means that other publishers have made a positive evaluation of your qualifications. Therefore, your chances of a favorable reception are even more likely.

As you progress in your career, and as your accomplishments become more significant, you often have less time to put together your resume. A readily available vita can work to your advantage. People seeking general information on your background and achievements can review your vita, which can later be augmented by a cover letter or personal interview.

2. : Locating or Changing Positions

> **COLLEGE PRESIDENT**- Catholic women's college seeks strong administrator with capacity for educational innovation, fund raising, and long-range campus planning. Experience in higher education is required and recruitment is open to men and women of any religious belief. Please reply with a cover letter and vita to chairman of search committee: William D. Brown, National Bank of Aberdeen, P. O. Box 3401 Aberdeen IA 56890-3401.

Employers and screening committees must have some way to quickly review the qualifications of large numbers of candidates for positions like the job above. For many openings, 100 or more vitas may be received.

To be considered for many jobs, your vita must make a strong first impression. Do not assume that the reader will know some things about you. Rather, <u>assume that the reader knows nothing about you, and every important item must be presented in the few pages of this professional document.</u>

3. : Updating Personnel Records

FINANCIAL AID PLANNER- Statewide higher education system recruiting a Coordinator of Financial Aid Planning. Successful candidate must have practical experience at the college level, plus executive and writing skills. Position available immediately or at the end of the school year. Send cover letter and complete information to Janice Mills, Personnel Director, State Education Agency, Old Capitol Building, Susex, NH 02156-3001.

Many organizations include in their personnel policies statements like the following:

> It is a policy of the Department of the Community Colleges that each faculty, staff, and administrative employee annually update the following items: employment application, transcripts of graduate work, and vita. A copy of these materials should be on file in the department chairperson's office and the Dean of Instruction's office.
>
> (Source: a community college handbook)

Such policies help ensure that information about your activities gets included in institutional annual reports. Data in these reports may be used by administrative officers who may not even know you. Where yearly updating is not required, you may volunteer a revised and updated vita for your personal file to help ensure the fullest review of your qualifications. This could increase your opportunities for promotion or special assignments and give you a competitive advantage over those who do vot update their vitas. More importantly, personnel records are routinely reviewed by employing organizations to identify candidates for jobs such as the financial planner advertised above. More and more employers are conducting annual performance reviews and the vita serves as the basis for the yearly personnel evaluation.

4. : Responding to Public Announcements

MANAGEMENT TRAINEE- Good Life Insurance Company is seeking qualified applicants for Management Trainee openings. Applicants should have a background in business administration, business management, or accounting. Relocation will follow training program. Send letter of interest and Vita to: Director of Employee Training, Good Life Insurance Company, 206 Main Street, Newburg, IN 40217-6752. Equal Opportunity and Affirmative Action Employer.

A basic tenet of affirmative-action programs is the requirement for full disclosure of all employment opportunities, which makes a strong vita and resume all the more important. The federal Equal Employment Opportunity Commission and its state and local counterparts feel that the "old" system of not announcing vacancies tended to perpetuate existing employment patterns-- patterns which often excluded minorities and women. Formerly, corporation executives, college presidents, or agency administrators were selected on the basis of informal personal recommendations from executive search firms, academic deans, or from employee personnel records. Now, these positions must be advertised publicly. Thanks to "sunshine laws," there has been a tremendous increase in publicly announced positions.

The move toward public announcement of jobs is highly desirable from an affirmative-action standpoint, but it has also greatly increased competition. Hundreds of vitas and resumes may now be submitted in response to a single listing--making a good professional summary even more important.

5. : Re-entering the Labor Market

MATURE WORKER National franchiser seeking
managerial workers needed for mature people seeking
change in work setting. Will operate this business after
free company orientation course in your own community.
Apply to Box 2000, Boston Globe, Boston, MA 76332-3232.

A professional summary is particularly important for people who are
returning to the job market after interrupting their careers to raise a family or to
go on an extended volunteer assignment. People who are laid off or expect to be
during a company downsizing will also need a resume. Their professional
summaries may emphasize skills and knowledge obtained through volunteer
work, part-time employment, credit or non credit continuing education, travel,
civic or political activities, participation in social organizations or other leisure
activity. A quality professional summary may be a passport to a variety of career
options. With computer technology virtually accessible to anyone seeking
employment, professional summaries can easily be revised to meet any
professional need. There are electronic scanners that sort out applications. Job
seekers read job descriptions carefully and include key words and language
similar to a position description. Often position descriptions are valuable to
professional summary writers. More information about specific professional
summary wording can be found in Chapter 9 of this book about electronic
resumes.

The same technique may be necessary for those who have been steadily
employed and now seek a change in career direction. Often, people at mid-life or
considering retirement may not necessarily want a promotion but rather a

change of work setting. Many who have not needed a professional summary for years now find a good vita essential to a desired career objective.

In summary, keen competition currently exists for almost all jobs and professional assignments. Employers receive dozens and sometimes hundreds of vitaes in response to a job listing. Your professional summary must make a positive impression on reviewers--and instantly.

Chapter 3

Gathering the Facts for a Professional Summary

There are three important steps for developing an effective professional summary: (1) compiling all potentially useful information--getting started; (2) selecting and assembling the key information--building the various sections in your best draft; and (3) outside reviewing and fine drafting information--putting the finished product together. This chapter and the next will help in compiling, assembling, and organizing your information. Chapter 4 will help you develop a portfolio using sample worksheets to put vital information in one place.

ASSOCIATION EXECUTIVE-National organization of flight crew attendants seeks top administrator. Must know transportation industry and be experienced in negotiations and collective bargaining. Congressional liaison, writing experience, and public speaking also important. Will direct a staff of 18, located in Virginia suburb of Washington, DC Apply P. O. Drawer D, Dulles Airport Station, VA 23695-1212. Resume and cover letter should be received by December 15.

Getting Started

The all-important first step in developing a professional summary is to <u>collect all relevant material</u>, then to organize it into broad categories. In the early stages it is best to assemble anything that might be used--better to start with too much than too little. Later, you can cut back when considering specific purposes or length. Too often, however, only selective information is gathered and the resulting vita fails to be as complete and comprehensive as it could be. For example, you might want to apply for a job requiring specific academic specialization, so you need to collect information from as many sources as possible for as many purposes as seem reasonable.

Here are some hints for each of the six major categories.

1.   **Personal Contact Information**--Where applicable, list both a business and home address with phone numbers, including voice mail if available, e-mail addresses, and fax numbers, if you have them--usually on opposite sides at the top of the page. However, if you are searching for a job and do not want your current employer or work contacts to know, use only your home address centered on the page or against the left margin. If you are a student, try to list a day-time contact, such as a department office or other place where you can receive messages or faxes. How you present your information is a matter of personal choice, so use the format which looks best to you. A job title is customarily included in the business address, if you have one. The general advice about including information on your vita is to include the personal information you feel is positive and not include any information that a screener might perceive as negative. The top of the vita might appear as:

Sarah Jones Smith

Assistant Professor
Department of Biology
Farwestern College
Las Vegas, Nevada 86400-0502
(913) 123-8867 (voice mail)
(913) 123-8079 Fax

711 Lucky Lane
Las Vegas, Nevada 86402-0008
(913) 123-4567 Tel/fax
E-Mail ssmith@farwes.edu

2.   **Educational Information**--In assembling information in this category, include all degree work as well as any related, significant educational activities. The key question is "What is significant?" If a person has a bachelor's, master's, and doctor's degree, then only the most significant of all other educational

experiences should be listed. For example, if the biologist noted below had attended a post doctoral institute in ecological studies, closely related to her professional qualifications, she probably want a prospective employer to know about it. In the final analysis, it is a matter of <u>taste and judgment</u>. Do not list so much that the section looks cluttered, but list what is important about your background. Ask yourself, "What do I want the reader to know?"

In gathering material, be sure you have copies of your transcripts as well as any related workshop, seminar or other extended study periods, especially those granting Continuing Education Units (CEU's).

An educational entry should normally include the name of the institution, location and zip code, degree awarded, dates, and field of study. If another field of study is significant, it may also be listed, but this is optional. For your professional portfolio you should have your own set of institutional transcripts because they are frequently requested. Increasingly they are. Also optional is the order in which the entry is laid out. A sample entry may look something like the following:

University of Pennsylvania, Philadelphia, Pennsylvania,
Ph.D., 1996 Major: Biology

University of Maryland, College Park, Maryland, M. S. 1993
Major: Biology

Bridgewater College, Bridgewater, Virginia, B. S., 1991
Major: General Science

3. **Employment Experience**--Several important points should be kept in mind when developing this section.

First, be sure to distinguish between part-time and full-time employment by using appropriate headings. This may seem like a simple suggestion, but it is often neglected and often misunderstood by the reader. A young person just starting out may have to show more part-time employment than a seasoned professional with a long history of full-time jobs. Special attention should be given to part-time employment which relates to work goals such as graduate research, teaching, assistantships, etc. The important thing is to show the skills and accomplishments that makes an entry important. Those with significant volunteer or other significant leisure activities may include them here rather than under civic or service activities. The key again is significance. For example, a volunteer job such as a district political party chairman would have career significance for a political scientist, but less so for a chemist. Be sure to show consulting activities here, if there are any. This is a section where if you have a strong background of work and leisure accomplishments, they can stand out. Have a clear vision of the purpose of each version of your vita as you put it together, but when getting started, put everything on your worksheets.

Second, the list should start with the current or most recent employment. Be certain to give the dates and your job title along with your employer's name and address, zip code and phone number in your worksheets. Other information may include major duties, areas of particular success or achievement, research interest, committee assignments, etc.   Entries should be uniform in length--not running downhill with a lot of information in recent entries and very little in later ones.

A frequent dilemma for veteran workers who have changed jobs or occupations or who have extremely long employment histories is just how much to list. The best rule of thumb is to list what is important for your purpose and summarize the rest. For example, if you worked in several industries as an engineer for ten years, then returned to a university for an MBA, and later a PhD. in business to go into college teaching, you may wish to summarize the industry and present individual entries for the most recent business teaching assignments.

Often you will need to emphasize a certain part of your professional experience such as the job listing below--so be sure to begin by including complete information in your worksheets.

> **COOPERATIVE EXECUTIVE-** Southern Alabama cotton cooperative seeking administrative director. Must be familiar with cotton and the operations of a cooperative association. The ideal candidate will have worked for a similar organization. Job begins at $25,000 but Board is willing to consider candidates with a successful record at higher salary. Reply to P. O. 149, Hillsboro, AL 35986-0149.

4. **Professional Affiliations and Honors**

Entries should include the following:

- current memberships in professional organizations
- significant appointments/elections to positions or special honors from professional, business, educational or related organizations.
- past memberships should also be put on worksheets, but used only if needed to support a particular vita purpose.

The emphasis here should be on current activities, except where you have changed fields of work and want to show some earlier organizational activity. If you are heavily involved with professional associations, choose a select set of entries but list them on your worksheet for references purposes. A notation might follow that a detailed listing is available upon request, or simply that a selective account has been given. In this section, as in others, <u>taste and good judgment along with clear organizational structure must be used</u>. Do not overload your vita with unimportant to insignificant details to the point of making the reader feel put down or put on.

5.   **Publications and Other Creative Works**- For many people this is a kind of catch-all category, a chance to show professional accomplishments. The usual items to be included in this section are as follows:

<u>Publications</u>- normally the most recent listed first.

Books, monographs, chapters

Periodicals--note if referred or non-referred

Book Reviews--list the publications where they appeared

Technical Papers, research reports, unpublished staff or internal

documents, curriculum materials (charts, graphs, posters), etc.

<u>Presentations</u>-

Paintings or graphics--note if juried shows

Exhibitions or concerts--solo or in groups

Speeches, lectures, panel appearances, workshop leadership

Dance or music recitals or workshops

<u>Media Presentations</u>-

Radio, television, and video appearances

Films, and film presentations

Records, tapes, and compact disc

Computer media

Courses developed for TV

<u>Inventions</u>-

Discoveries, development of new procedures or techniques

Patents or copyrights

Software developed

For publications, show full bibliographic entries so that a reader can easily find them. For senior professionals, who may have a very long list of publications, it is sometimes appropriate to use a phrase such as the following:

"Partial listing--a complete listing is available upon request."

"Selected listing--a full listing available upon request."

"Entries only since 1980--a complete list will be sent on request."

6.   **Civic, Religious or Service Activities-** This section should be similar to the one on professional affiliations--primarily a listing of significant activities. Since this is a professional document, the entries should be made judiciously, with brevity the key. Avoid those of lesser significance. For some people in business and industry, this is an important area of work-related involvement and may deserve a more detailed account than for professionals in other settings. Long-term activities, particularly those of leadership or team nature or important service activities such as service on a board of directors or elected office, should be shown in this section.

Your experience in community action activities, for example, could be very helpful in applying for the position cited below.

> **DIRECTOR, WOMEN'S CENTER-** Newly-established center to provide educational and career counseling for women seeks a director. Must be experienced in both counseling and administration and be able to develop an effective fund-raising program. Job might be filled on a part-time basis. Send cover letter and vita to Professor Elizabeth Mills, Westmoreland College, Westmoreland, MI 67809-1432.

6.   **Other Optional Items-** Some areas exist that simply do not fit into these general categories. Examples include the following:

- computer skills--of growing importance
- foreign language skills or overseas residence--important in today's global economy
- courses taught or created and media used
- institutional committee responsibilities
- dissertations and theses direction/advising
- research and development activities and grants
- creative writing outside your professional field
- hobbies or important leisure activities and skills

Each of these and others like them, may grow out of your particular experience and can be placed in the vita with a suitable heading. Teachers may not consider it necessary to show courses that have been taught for a vita going to a non-education related employer. Yet, for introductory purposes, information about leisure activities may be of special interest. So the rule of thumb is first to collect all the data on your worksheets that might fit this particular purpose and to decide later how to use those accomplishments that make you unique and stand apart from others. If you have strengths here, put them in your worksheets and use them in your vita when appropriate.

One of the most difficult things for veteran professionals is updating professional summaries. In the busy pace of work, it is easy to forget items, even important ones. The best way to avoid this is to maintain a special file each year-- 1996, 1997, 1998, etc., containing items to be used when revising or updating your summary. This yearly file should contain such items as the following:

- significant educational accomplishments--keep CEU's
- new or modified job assignments--keep announcements
- appointments, committees, or appointment to offices
- funded or special projects--keep award letters
- published work or other creative activities--keep copies
- significant speeches or participation in key meetings
- special recognition
- new important professional affiliations--keep licensure numbers here

A good time to revise and update a general purpose vita is each January. This provides you with an opportunity for an annual review of your activities while they are fresh in your mind, rather than waiting several years to bring the material up to date.

Current vs. Past Information

Under the pressure of adding new material, a never-ending battle will be fought over what should remain in a vita and what to take out. Certainly, currentness is a key factor in any personal summary. There should always be a date somewhere on the vita, usually at the very end. Information including address, phone number and job title should be kept current at all times. Never send a copy out which is not accurate in these important items or, worse, with handwritten changes. A review group was formally considering a candidate who submitted a vita clearly using a home address that was two years out of date. The readers knew this and could only assume the preparer had not updated other material and dropped the person from serious consideration.

This sort of problem can easily be avoided by keeping the vita timely. If certain entries are beginning to get lengthy and old, then it is entirely appropriate to make notations such as :

"This is a sample of publications; a complete list is available on request."
"These are selected grants and contracts received since 1990; a complete list is available upon request."
"This is a list of dissertations directed only since 1992; a complete list is available upon request."
"Work experience prior to 1990 was in the field of retail sales; a complete list of these positions will be furnished upon request."

The central point is to keep the vita looking fresh and timely, which requires dropping old or less important material with appropriate notations such as the ones above. Of course, you must make sure not to leave time in this house-cleaning activity. As always, good judgment and taste should serve as the final determinant. Keep in mind that this is your document and you can pick and choose what to present--unless an employer specifies certain information must be included.

Style

Entries are usually cryptic in nature. Do not use a pure narrative format unless it suits your purpose to emphasize a particular skill. This means using brief annotations or listings with few, if any, complete sentences. There should be a heavy emphasis on action verbs to describe your skills and accomplishments. Both block (square) or indented styles may be used as long as one or the other is used consistently through out the vita. Publication entries should follow a consistent style such as University of Chicago's Press, <u>The Chicago Manual of Style</u> or the <u>Publication Manual of the American Psychological Association</u>[2]. The objective is to keep the style open and easily readable with wide margins and plenty of open space. Make it attractive to the reader so it will be picked out by a committee as the most interesting vita--or least tedious. Your writing skills and organizational ability are being judged along with the content of your background. Therefore, an attractive, well-written, and fact-filled vita or resume can give your career a big boost.

Headings

<u>Careful use of headings is one of the keys to a successful vita.</u> It provides the opportunity to organize material around certain topics. The usual headings have been cited earlier in this chapter. Others can be added as necessary in areas of special experience, competence, or strength.

Subheadings may also be used to highlight some particular activity, such as part-time or volunteer work related to professional goals. Sub-headings may be used, for example, in a "Publications and Special Creations" section to emphasize any unique writing, art, innovation, or editing which merits citation. The same is true for significant involvement in organizations like the League of Women Voters, the National Association for the Advancement of Colored People (NAACP), Jaycees, American Association of University Women (AAUW), Rotary, etc.

Headings can also improve the look of the Vita. Use them to your best advantage--this means not cluttering your page with too many of them. If you use one, be sure you have at least two entries listed under it.

AGENCY DIRECTOR- Newly funded program serving the handicapped seeks experienced administrator to plan and direct an 18-month project. Must have appropriate training and experience. Salary range $25,000 to $28,000, but negotiable. Reply to Director, Community Services Agency, 400 S. Main Street, North Holland, WI 48673-1662 by sending a cover letter, vita with references.

References

Should you list references? For a general purpose vita or resume, generally do not include references. Once again, this is purely a matter of judgment and taste. The deciding factors are who will read the vita and what use will they make of it. References would be important, for example, for candidates for the above job. If you decide to show references, whom should you include? Again that depends mainly on how you intend to use the vita. Usually you will want to cite two or three professional supervisors and a person who knows your work as a colleague, and perhaps someone who knows your most recent academic work.

You might cite references where their names alone would be of special help and make your application stand out. For example, if you were applying for a college coaching job and were able to list coaches at Notre Dame, Illinois, and Stanford as references--do it.

A list of references would probably not be appropriate for seeking a promotion within the same institution. However, if you are applying for a new position 2,000 miles away as a sales manager or production supervisor, then a list of references could be extremely helpful--especially if you are not sending credentials.

The rule of thumb, then, is to list three to six references if the vita is to be used for changing jobs. A long list of six to ten names is usually not necessary. A note that additional references will be furnished upon request can cover other names if desired. If references are used, the entry for each person should include name, address, job title, organization, and current business phone number, fax number and e-mail address, if applicable. Of course, you should follow the usual courtesy of asking people if you may list them <u>before you enter their names</u>. And it is very smart to give them a copy of your vita to help jog their memory concerning your achievements and appropriate background.

Credentials

Many people feel that credentials, as defined in Chapter 1, are indispensable when seeking a position in the field of education. Some employers insist on having them sent as a part of the initial application process, while others want them later. Try to keep a set of credentials with the placement office at one of the institutions from which you have a degree. Some universities are cutting back on this service--be sure to ask. If this is not possible or convenient, a private placement agency will usually offer the same service for a fee. Occasionally, a college or university placement office will establish a credentials file for non-alumni, usually for a fee. If you need to have such a file and are having trouble getting started, check with a convenient college placement office director. If requested, the office having your credentials on file may let you know when a job in your area opens up.

Chapter 4

Building and Maintaining a Professional Portfolio

In recent years people of all ages have become interested in eatablishing a portfolio. For the professional a portfolio is especially important for several reasons:

It is a convenient way of recording certain key professional information.

It provides a motion picture of your professional accomplishments each year over a period of time.

It is a way of gathering vital information in building and maintaining a professional summary.

It provides a way to do an annual review of your accomplishments as a part of a January career development check-up.

It is a place to keep copies of professional letters, papers, certificates, publications, presentations, evaluations, etc.

Your professional portfolio may be as simple as a file folder or elaborate as an artist case of original works. Over time back-up data may occupy half a file drawer or considerable shelf space. Whether your portfolio is large or small, it is a way to provide material on the professional summary worksheets to help put your vita together. You may want to use a professionally developed type such as the Life Work Portfolio, available from the Oklahoma Department of Vocational Technical Education, Stillwater, OK 74074-4364; (800) 654-4502.

You may find occasions when you want to take your professional portfolio with you on interviews to show illustrations of your publications, reprints of articles, reports or papers that you have presented.

Professional Summary Worksheets

To help you develop a base of information for use when filling out a professional vita or resume, follow the set of work sheets provided. You may wonder why it is important to fill out this long list of items about yourself. The evidence shows that, too often, busy people forget what they have done or cannot recall full details about their activities at the time they prepare a professional summary. Also, if you have a complete written summary of your total qualifications available, persons asked to critique your vita can help make sure that you included the important items or presented them in the most advantageous way.

Your worksheets need not be kept in "photocopy" condition as they will not be sent to any outsiders--except those advising you on how to improve your vita. You will want to write in new developments or make marginal inserts. Periodically, when it gets too hard to read, a general revision is in order. There is an extra set of worksheets at the end of the book--they can be copied for future use.

It is always better to err on the side of including too much data in your worksheets rather than too little. Use a cryptic style to save space. But make sure that enough detail remains to jog your memory and to make sure you can recall the highest level of achievement or any special recognition or accomplishment.

Add extra sections to the worksheets in areas that do not seem to fully include your particular background. These should be considered a starting point--not an ending.

Another way to keep these worksheets up to date is to keep this information on a computer disc, if that is convenient and practical.

Professional Portfolio Worksheets

Name   Date Prepared or Updated

                                            Social Security Number

Present Address:

_____

P. O. Box or Street

_____

City

_____

State   Zip Code

_____

Phone (Area Code)   Fax (Area Code)

_____

e-mail Address

Business Address

_____

Employed by (organization or institution)

_____

Job Title

_____

Phone (Area Code)   Fax (Area Code)

_____

P. O. Box or Street

_____

State   Zip Code

_____

e-mail Address

Permanent Address (if same above leave blank)

_____

P. O. Box or Street

_____

City

_____

State   Zip Code

_____

Phone (Area Code)   Fax (Area Code)

_____

e-mail Address

Other Personal Information

_____

Birthplace   Birth Date

_____

Military Service Branch (if any)   Length of Service

_____

Title and Military Occupational Specialty Code

_____

Highest Rank Obtained   Awards

_____

Special Schools Completed

_____

Transferable Skills Obtained

Educational Background (begin with most recent first)

Degree	Date Graduated	Transcripts

Major		Minor

Institution

Location		Zip Code

Notes (Special honors or recognition)

Degree	Date Graduated	Transcripts

Major		Minor

Institution

Location		Zip Code

Notes (Special honors or recognition)

Degree   Date Graduated   Transcripts

Major   Minor

Institution

Location   Zip Code

Notes (Special honors or recognition)

Degree   Date Graduated   Transcripts

Major   Minor

Institution

Location   Zip Code

Notes (Special honors or recognition)

Other Training

(It is important to note yearly updates and times as well as Continuing Education Units (CEU's), if appropriate. Include any independent study.

_____

_____

_____

Employment Information

Work History (include full-time employment, internships, etc.--start with current position)

_____
Position Title: Dates

_____
Employer

_____
Location   Zip Code

_____
Supervisor   Title

_____
Specific Responsibilities and Accomplishments

_____

Position Title: _____ **Dates** _____

Employer _____

Location _____ **Zip Code** _____

Supervisor _____ **Title** _____

Specific Responsibilities and Accomplishments _____

_____

_____

_____

Position Title: _____ **Dates** _____

Employer _____

Location _____ **Zip Code** _____

Supervisor _____ **Title** _____

Specific Responsibilities and Accomplishments _____

_____

_____

_____

_____

Position Title: Dates

Employer

Location   Zip Code

Supervisor   Title

Specific Responsibilities and Accomplishments

_____

_____

_____

Position Title: Dates

Employer

Location   Zip Code

Supervisor   Title

Specific Responsibilities and Accomplishments

_____

_____

_____

Position Title: _____ Dates _____

Employer _____

Location _____ Zip Code _____

Supervisor _____ Title _____

Specific Responsibilities and Accomplishments _____

_____

_____

_____

Position Title: _____ Dates _____

Employer _____

Location _____ Zip Code _____

Supervisor _____ Title _____

Specific Responsibilities and Accomplishments _____

_____

_____

Other Employment (Include in this section part-time employment and jobs held during summer vacations, holidays, etc., and other employment not listed

in the previous section. When doing this for the first time be sure to get your dates and records clear, then use only as it seems appropriate--if at all in your vita.)

_____

_____

_____

_____

_____

_____

_____

Spouse's Work

_____

_____

_____

Special Competencies (include teaching areas, artistic talents, organizational skills, supervisory skills, public speaking skills, sales ability, proposals funded, etc.)

_____

_____

_____

_____

Other Personal Data

_____

_____

_____

Certification or License Status with numbers and date issued

License	Authority	Expiration date
License	Authority	Expiration date

Computer Skills- Include knowledge of major applications such as desk top publishing, spreadsheets, and word processing and/or database and programming skills.

_____

_____

_____

_____

Professional and Civic Activities

Memberships in professional associations (include both the name of the organizations and offices you hold or have held with dates. Also, any significant activities completed under your leadership.)

_____

_____

_____

_____

Professional and Civic Activities cont.

_____

_____

_____

_____

_____

_____

Religious Affiliation and Activities--including elected and appointed positions and dates

_____

_____

_____

_____

Community Services Activities--including appointed and elected positions with dates

_____

_____

_____

_____

_____

_____

_____

Leisure Activities--such as hobbies and volunteer involvement--note skills, special responsibilities, elected or appointed leadership duties.

_____

_____

_____

Foreign Languages--note written and spoken skill levels as well as major international travel or residence, note any special courses, training, and self-taught knowledge acquired.

_____

_____

_____

_____

Creative Professional Activities (include articles, books, reports, inventions, copyrights, or patents, paintings, poetry, music or plays written, exhibits displayed, etc.)

_____

_____

_____

_____

_____

Awards and Honors

Special Interests and Notes

References

Name

Position

Address

Phone   Date confirmed

Fax   Date confirmed

Name

Position

Address

Phone   Date confirmed

Fax   Date confirmed

Name _____

Position _____

Address _____

Phone _____ Date confirmed _____

Fax _____ Date confirmed _____

Name _____

Position _____

Address _____

Phone _____ Date confirmed _____

Fax _____ Date confirmed _____

Name
_____

Position
_____

Address
_____

Phone _____ Date confirmed _____

Fax _____ Date confirmed _____

Name
_____

Position
_____

Address
_____

Phone _____ Date confirmed _____

Fax _____ Date confirmed _____

Note: Select from this listing three to five to use in the actual vita, if requested at an interview.

Chapter 5

Putting the Vita Together

Now that you have collected all of your background material and have brought your professional development worksheets up to date, you are ready to put your vita together.

Before you start to develop your vita, consider the following points. They are much easier to address before you prepare your first draft because if they are not followed, they will tend to distract even the critic readers from appreciating your qualifications. That's right--critic readers. It is suggested in this book that one of the keys to a successful vita is the use of able critic readers. More about this later.

The essential issues in putting all of the facts you have collected together in some kind of meaningful document can be summed up in three words:

CLARITY
CONSISTENCY
CONCISENESS

Stressing these three points will put you well on the way to producing the best possible vita.

CLARITY

Most people who read your vita <u>will not know you</u>. Therefore, you must communicate a clear impression about yourself--your background and your qualifications and accomplishments. So keep in mind that <u>you are writing this</u>

document <u>mainly for strangers</u> whom you need to inform. The only way you can really communicate your assets is to describe your important previous activities in the clearest fashion possible. Probably the worst thing that can happen to your vita is for any reader to feel "it is confusing." Your vita may be read (or scanned) along with 30 or 40 others in an hour by an individual or a committee responsible for developing a list of candidates for employment or promotion. It has to be clear and understandable--the first time. If you were applying for the job cited below, you would have to be precise and specific.

> **MARKET ANALYST-** Large diversified advertising agency seeks recent MBA graduate with some course work in market research or advertising for staff position. Prefer some experience, but will consider persons with generally strong qualifications. Please reply to Box 157, NEW YORK SUN.

To ensure an accurate presentation of your qualifications, avoid the four frequent errors cited below:

1. **Lack of Clarity** on Educational Background
    This seems so fundamental, but many people leave off key   items such as:

    - major area of concentration
    - year degree received
    - be sure to show the official name of the degree
    - complete name of institution, including zip code
    - location of institution, especially if the namemay be the same or similar to another institution

2. **Lack of Clarity** on Employment History

Dates, sequence of activities, job titles and duties, and history can confuse the readers. Clarity can be maintained if a few simple rules are followed:

- be sure to show periods of full-time student status under a separate sub-heading
- be sure to leave no gaps in years worked or studied (account for every year)
- be sure to show employer, job title, and dates starting with the most recent.
- be sure to distinguish between full-time, part time, and summer work
- be sure to use separate headings for such enteries as:

    military service

    volunteer activities
- be sure to account for leaves of absence (be sure to explain)

3. **Lack of Clarity** on Professional Activities

Failure to be clear in this area may mislead the reader, such as showing association activities that are not current. This may seem harmless, but the reader may know, by chance, that you are not currently in this role and may discount your entire vita. The same thing may be true for offices held in the past, appointed positions, etc. To avoid all of this confusion:

- current memberships
- show date clearly on all former activities and memberships
- omit former leisure activities which do not materially aid your current qualifications or which are equivalent to current assignments.

- be prepared to document elected or appointed posts if required to do so.

Most of the problems in this area are careless rather than capricious, so take some extra care to make certain that enteries are clear and accurate.

4.   **Lack of Clarity** on Publications or Creative Works

A frequent problem in this area is not clarifying your role in a group effort, such as joint authorships, co-directing a research and development project, collaborative presentation, etc. Another difficulty can be encountered when you do not distinguish between refereed (reviewed by an editorial board) and non-refereed journals--as expected in some places of employment. Also, regarding publications, if there are a large number of items, it is usually best to use separate headings for various types, such as journal articles, books, chapters in books, monographs, pamphlets, etc. The same care should be taken when developing sections for inventions, patents, paintings, and other artistic works.

CONSISTENCY

Consistency is vital to show clear organization and to help the rapid reader. If a reader finds inconsistencies, he or she might conclude that:

The person is careless.
The person does not know how to prepare a vita.
The person may be trying to confuse the reader.

None of these conclusions are necessarily true and simple attention to details can eliminate this problem area. Here are some key points to follow:

Do not mix styles in any category.

Do not show double entries.

Do not mix chronological orders, such as last, first, last..

1. Do not mix styles in any category. For example if you are annotating entries under the work history, then do it for all enteries--be consistent. Likewise, show who was the senior project officer or inventor for all activities, not just a few. In short, leave no doubt what you did at every point in your vita.

2. Do not make double entries. This means do not list a publication or presentation more than once. Some people make the mistake of believing that multiple citations strengthen their vita by creating the impression of professional productivity. For example, a person may deliver a paper at a professional meeting that is also published as a part of its proceedings. Then it may be accepted for publication in a professional journal or is accepted for inclusion in a book of readings. This illustration is about one effort on the part of the person. If it is listed in a publications entry, it should be noted that it was previously entered as a paper, in conference proceedings, in a book of readings, etc. In short, make sure the reader knows your record shows consistency and honesty.

The same thing can happen for an entry under part-time work, which includes a graduate assistantship under work, but, later, also cites it under "Honors or Awards." Show it in one place, but not both. Likewise, reports of research projects should be listed only once--either under "Publications" or "Research Projects"--not under both.

3. Do not mix chronological orders. Again, many people botch up this simple point. Review your background data and decide how the information can be presented best, i.e. most recent first or last, then stay with that order in all

section. Most persons elect to begin with the current employment and highest degree first. That is, enter your most recent degree earned first under "Educational Background," if there is more than one. Also, enter your latest position or current if you are employed full-time, first under your work history section. Follow it with prior positions in descending chronological order, ending up with your first job. Do the same thing for part-time or volunteer work under separate headings. If this is the order you want to use, then follow it with publications or creative works, professional activities, etc.

CONCISENESS

The key principle here can be expressed very simply: Do not pad! As the creator and subject of your vita, you may have trouble knowing when to stop including all the important things you have done and go beyond the barrier of good judgment and taste. Remember, however, that after a certain level of detail, it may be best to summarize or highlight information rather than continuing on and on. For example, instead of listing the title of every article you have ever published in the last 20 to 25 years, perhaps an entry following those published in four or five years might read something like this:

"A complete list of 55 articles and books published between 1970-1990 will be furnished upon request."

The same line of reasoning may be appropriate for professional activities, creative works, and the like.

Be concise within each category and in the aggregate. While there is no magic maximum number of pages, most authorities agree that 10 pages is probably long enough for any vita. Obviously, there could be some extenuating circumstances which might warrant going beyond this point--but not far. Ideally, six to eight pages is probably about right for most veteran professionals, which means merging and summarizing some categories. It is really a matter of what you are trying to report about your professional self. When length becomes an issue, you may need to prioritize and eliminate some content. For a young professional, a two to four page vita should communicate the essential background details. For a seasoned worker who has been very active professionally, it may take 6. 8. to 10 pages to report what you feel needs to be stated.

Slanting Selected Material

A specific type of vita format is used in this book. <u>This should, however, be considered one of several optional formats.</u> Almost endless variations can be played on this theme. <u>The real direction should come from how you see the material being used and who will be reading it.</u> For example if you are applying for a university post but are currently working for the federal government while teaching part-time for a local college, it would be important to stress the teaching responsibilities you carry as well as your volunteer work advising students. Both of these items would receive only minor attention on a vita prepared for state government employment. By the same token, if the vita is geared toward a research and development firm, you may want to stress your grants management, proposal review, and technical writing experience.

Ms. A---Associate Professor
Applying for Three Jobs at The Same Time
What Should She Stress?

Worksheet Data (Using only Selected examples)	Job A Assistant Dean at another University	Job B Full Professorship at same institution	Job C Member, National Board for her church
Participation in Post-doctoral research	Cite	Describe Highly Relevant	Probably Omit
Teaching Experience	Describe	Describe in Detail	Cite
Member, Board of Directors, Campus International House	Describe	Describe in Detail	Describe Highly Relevant
Research Activities and Publications	Describe	Describe Highly Relevant	Omit
Foreign Travel	Cite	Cite	Describe Highly Relevant
Service on Faculty Senate Committee	Describe	Describe Highly Relevant	Cite
Church Membership	Omit	Omit	Cite
Leadership in Church Service Activities	Cite	Describe	Describe Highly Relevant
Leadership in Civic/Service Activities	Cite	Describe	Describe
Academic Honors and Awards	Describe	Describe Highly Relevant	Cite or Omit
Professional Association Activities	Cite	Describe Highly Relevant	Cite or Omit

Leisure Activities and Special Interests	Omit	Cite	Describe

The vita is your document: Make it work for you!
Do not feel that one version will serve all purposes. For example, you do not want to hear later that you might have gotten the position except no one knew about your conference planning activities--one of your special skill areas. Some people have a vita they use for introductions before speeches, another version used for grant and contract proposals, and a third when applying for a new position. In short, know your readers and what uses they will make of a vita. Then, develop it to suit their purposes from your perspective.

Outside Readers or Critic Readers

Outside readers can provide very helpful advice about your professional summaries. Lawyers do not advise themselves on legal matters and psychologists do not try to prescribe their own therapy. In the same way, you will probably be too close and too involved in the final product to critically review your own vita and make the necessary changes. Furthermore, you know the content so well that all of the information seems clear and makes sense to you--but may not be so for other readers.

For the best results, three kinds of outside readers are suggested:

1.   A professional friend who knows you and your work well enough to spot significant missing information or points that are confusing.

2.   A professional person who does not know you well, who will read critically as a person learning about you for the first time. Since this will be the status of most of your eventual readers, this is an important choice. Pick someone who will find faults if there are any and will tell you about them--rather than a person who will not take the assignment seriously or who will be too afraid of offending you.

3.   A hiring or personnel officer that you know. For someone in business and industry, this might be a personnel officer. For someone in higher education this might be a dean or department head. The key is to use someone experienced in reviewing vitaes   for both promotions and for new employment.

If possible, these three readers should review your nearly final or absolute final draft--one which you think has all of the rough spots ironed out and is ready for professional use. You will not receive their best efforts unless you first present them with your best effort. Do not bother them with early efforts that you know need polishing. When you receive their comments, don't be defensive about the points they raise. Objectively evaluate their suggestions and take full advantage of ideas that have merit. Make all of the changes that seem reasonable.

Sample Worksheets and Vitaes

A completed set of worksheets for Sarah F. Parker begins on the next page. The worksheets are the same as those appearing in Chapter 4, except they have been filled out to illustrate how data might be recorded. You can use the blank sample for your own notes and to update information as it becomes available. Her completed vita follows. Another sample vita for William Roberts closes this chapter. Some books present large numbers of sample summaries, except no one ever seems to find the one that fits them exactly. This book attempts to set forth basic principles and expects the good sense of the reader plus a few examples to help bridge the gap from general guidelines to the desired result.

Remember what you are really looking for in these samples is format and style, not content. Try to get a feel for how you want your vita to appear when you have it ready for final draft and critical review. Some parts of the format presented here might not fit your needs. If so, discard the portions you cannot use and add some of your own.

Professional Portfolio Worksheets

Present Address:

1234 First Avenue

P. O. Box or Street

Burtonsville

City

Arkansas   *50010-0001*

State   Zip Code

(501) 411-4321   *(501) 411-4322*

Phone (Area Code)   Fax (Area Code)

sparker@arkansas.edu

e-mail Address

Business Address

Riverside College

Employed by (organization or institution)

Associate Professor and Chairperson, Political Science Dept.

Job Title

(501) 411-2202   *(501) 411-2221*

Phone (Area Code)   Fax (Area Code)

1420 College Street

P. O. Box or Street

Arkansas   *50009-0003*

State   Zip Code

parker@riverside.edu.

e-mail Address

Permanent Address (if same above leave blank)

5876 Lane Street

P. O. Box or Street

Lexington

City

Kentucky   *40011-0002*

State   Zip Code

(606) 511-9876   *(606) 511-9889*

Phone (Area Code)   Fax (Area Code)

None

e-mail Address

Other Personal Information

Lexington, KY   *January 3, 1958*

Birthplace   Birth Date

Military Service Branch (if any)   Length of Service

Title and Military Occupational Specialty Code

Highest Rank Obtained   Awards

Special Schools Completed

Transferable Skills Obtained

Educational Background (begin with most recent first)

Ph.D.   *May, 1991*   *yes received 2/14/90*

Degree	Date Graduated	Transcripts

Political Science   *History*

Major	Minor

University of Arkansas

Institution

Fayetteville, Arkansas   *50000-3434*

Location	Zip Code

University of Arkansas Dissertation Award

Notes (Special honors or Recognition)

M. A.   *August, 1984*   *yes, received 2/17/90*

Degree	Date Graduated	Transcripts

Political Science   *History Cognate*

Major	Minor

George Washington University

Institution

Washington, D. C.   *20004-0004*

Location	Zip Code

Mostly part-time study, one of the few women in the program

Notes (Special honors or Recognition)

B. A. *June, 1980* *No, Requested 1/20/96*

Degree	Date Graduated	Transcripts

History *None*

Major		Minor

University Of Mississippi

Institution

Oxford, Mississippi *30041-1567*

Location	Zip Code

President, Constitution Club, Dean's List 3 terms, Young

Notes (Special honors or Recognition)

Democrats

Degree	Date Graduated	Transcripts

Major		Minor

Institution

Location	Zip Code

Notes (Special honors or Recognition)

Other Training

(It is important to note yearly update and times as well as Continuing Education Units (CEU's), if appropriate. Include independent study.

Workshop for Women in Leadership Positions in Higher

_____

Education, Sponsored by American Council on Higher

_____

Education, Conducted by American University, Wash. D. C.

_____

Summer of 78-79- non-credit Leadership Training Institute

for young Democrats, Louisville, KY.

Participated in KY Governor School, 1974-1976

Awarded $4,000 Competitive Scholarship.

Employment Information

Work History (include full-time employment, internships, etc.--start with current position

Associate Chairperson and Professor, Political Science 07/94-present

---

Position Title: Dates

Riverside College

Employer

College Town, Arkansas   *50099-0003*

Location   **Zip Code**

Liberty M. Jefferson, Ph.D. Dean, College of Arts and Sciences

---

Supervisor   **Title**

Perform chairperson duties, coordinate instruction and research

---

Specific Responsibilities and Accomplishments

activities of 3 persons. teach 2-3 classes per term, advise students.

Associate Professor, Political Science   8/87-6/94

Position Title: Dates

Riverside College

Employer

College Town, Arkansas   *50099-0009* Locatior

                                                     Zip Code

Thomas S. Paine, Ph.D.   *Chairperson, Dept. Political Science*

Supervisor   **Title**

Full-time professor, political science, usual load-4 classes.

Specific Responsibilities and Accomplishments

Adviser to 25 undergraduate political science majors.

Assistant Professor, Political Science, History   *8/85-6/87*

Position Title: **Dates**

University of Arkansas

Employer

Fayetteville, Arkansas   *50000-3434*

Location   **Zip Code**

John Jay, Ph.D.   *Chairman, Political Science & History Department*

Supervisor   **Title**

Taught full load of classes, Dept. of Political Science and History,

Specific Responsibilities and Accomplishments

Advisor to Political Science Majors, Served on various committees.

Administrative Assistant   *7/80-8/83*

Position Title: **Dates**

U. S. Congressman, Roy Turk

Employer

Rayburn Building- Washington, D. C   *20001-4444*

Location   **Zip Code** *The*

Honorable Roy Turk   *Congressman*

Supervisor   **Title**

Responsible for all office duties, dealt with constituents' requests

Specific Responsibilities and Accomplishments

-liaison person with other office assistants, drafted and typed legislation

70

Research Associate   *5/79-6/80*

Position Title: **Dates**

Governor of Mississippi

Employer

Jackson, Mississippi   *70001-1234*

Location   **Zip Code**

Benjamin North, Ph.D.   *Research Director*

Supervisor   **Title**

Worked on task force on governmental affairs associated with

Specific Responsibilities and Accomplishments

University, Collected data and helped draft final committee report.

Position Title: **Dates**

Employer

Location   **Zip Code**

Supervisor   **Title**

Specific Responsibilities and Accomplishments

71

Other Employment (Include in this section part-time employment and jobs held during summer vacations, holidays, etc., and other employment not listed in the previous section. When doing this for the first time be complete and get your dates and records clear, then use only as it seems appropriate--if at all in your vita.)

Summer 1988- Administrative Assistant to campaign manager

Successful Democratic Congressional Election, Arkansas 2nd District.

Summer 1984- Director of Summer Session for Gifted High School

Students. Fairfax City, Virginia

Summer 1979- Staff Assistant to Governmental Research Center.

University of Mississippi

Spouse's Work

CPA for the last 15 years

Special Competencies (include teaching areas, artistic talents, organizational skills, supervisory skills, public speaking skills, sales ability, proposals funded. etc.)

Speaking on: (1.) Women's Voting Rights (2.) Evolution and

Passage of the Nineteenth Amendment (3.) Political Contributions

of Women in American History. Teaching Fields: (1.) U. S.

Government, Local, State, Federal. (2.) Legislative Process (3).

Voter Behavior (4.) Sampling (5.) Special Interest Groups (6.)

Public Opinion. Active in local, state, and national elective campaigns.

Certification or License Status with numbers and date issued

None

License	Authority	Expiration date
License	Authority	Expiration date
License	Authority	Expiration date

Computer Skills- Include knowledge of major applications such as desk top publishing, spreadsheets, and word processing and/or database and programming skills.

Know Windows '95

_____

Know SPASS Statistical Program

_____

_____

_____

Professional and Civic Activities

Memberships in Professional Associations (include both the name of the associations and offices you hold or have held with dates. Also any significant activities completed under your leadership.)

Current: American Political Science Association

_____

American Association Of University Professors

_____

Organization of American Historians- Southwest Region

_____

_____

Professional and Civic Activities cont.

Past   AAUW

              National Education Association

Elected   Editorial Board Member-American Political Science Review

              Chairman, Legislative Liaison Committee of University

              of Arkansas Faculty, 1987.

Appointed: Special Committee to Study Voter Registration, Arkansas U.

Religious Affiliation and Activities--including elected and appointed positions and dates

Lifelong member- Methodist Church, Active in Women's Work,

President, Local Community Action Group 1989, Served on local board

of ministries 1985-88. Sunday School Teacher 1973-78.

Wesley Foundation Advisor, Riverside College

Community Services Activities--including appointed and elected positions with dates

Chairperson of Burtonsville, Arkansas Bicentennial Committee, 1992. Served on Governor's

Bicentennial Committee for the State of Arkansas, 1991-92.

_____

_____

_____

_____

Leisure Activities--such as hobbies and volunteer involvement- notes skills, special responsibilities, elected or appointed leadership duties.

Sports including swimming and tennis

_____

Sewing and candle-making

_____

Watching Political Activities on TV

_____

Politics, Reading, Women in Public Life

Foreign languages--note written and spoken skill levels as well as major international travel or residence, note any special courses, training, and self-taught knowledge acquired.

French - read and write -fluent

Spanish - read- some

Creative Professional Activities (include articles, books, reports, inventions, copyrights, or patents, paintings, poetry, music or plays written, exhibits displayed, etc.)

Parker, Sarah F. "Political Profiles of Selected Women in American History."
    Unpublished master's thesis, George Washington University,   Washington,
DC,   1984. Parker, Sarah F., "A Political Perspective of the Nineteenth
Amendment."
    Unpublished doctor's thesis, University of Arkansas, 1991.
Parker, Sarah F., "Women and Politics: A Historical Perspective." *American
Political   Science Review* (Bicentennial Issue), 14, 7, 1992.

Parker, Sarah F., "The Struggle for the Vote." *American Political Science
    Review,* 14, 3,   1990, pp. 22-32.
Parker, Sarah F., "First Women Officeholders in the South." *Tulane Political
    Quarterly,* 58, 1, 1988, pp. 17-24.

Awards and Honors

Alpha Chi Honor Society, University of Mississippi, 1978-1979

Cum Laude Graduate, University of Mississippi, 1980

Forensics Scholarship, University of Mississippi, 1978

Nominee Fullbright Scholarship, 1983

Special Interests and Notes

Participation of Women in Politics/Past, Present and Future

Voter Registration

Maximizing Efficiency in Governmental Operations

Political Perspectives on Important Historical Events

Legislative Process

International Travel with Congressman

References

Dr. B. F. Simmons

Name

President, Riverside College

Position

College Town, AK   5001-0002

Address

(501) 411-2202	*10/96*

Phone	**Date confirmed**
(501) 411-2204	*10/96*

Fax	**Date confirmed**

Dr. Iris Martin, Dean

Name

College of Arts and Sciences, Assistant Dean

Position

College Town, AK 50011-0002

Address

(501) 411-2202	*10/96*

Phone	**Date confirmed**
(501) 411-2204	*10/96*

Fax	**Date confirmed**

Dr. Sarah S. Jones

Name

President, Faculty Senate, Riverside College

Position

College Town, AK 50001-0002

Address

(501) 411-2202	*10/96*
Phone	**Date confirmed**
(501) 411-2204	*10/96*
Fax	**Date confirmed**

Professor Jane Powell

Name

Professor, Department of Political Science, University of Arkansas

Position

University of Arkansas, Fayetteville, AK 50010-0002

Address

(501) 777-8832	*9/94*
Phone	**Date confirmed**
(501) 777-8838	*9/94*
Fax	**Date confirmed**

80

Dr. Jane L. Smith

Name

Dean, College of Social Sciences, George Washington University

Position

The George Washington University, Washington, D. C. 20017-0001

Address

(202) 788-4000	*7/93*
Phone	**Date confirmed**
(202) 788-4004	*7/93*
Fax	**Date confirmed**

J. P. "Pete" Adams

Name

Lawyer, Chairman State Democratic Party, Arkansas

Position

1237 Logan Street Little Rock, AK 50273-0004

Address

(501) 727-4379	*2/94*
Phone	**Date confirmed**
(501) 727-4729	*2/94*
Fax	**Date confirmed**

Note: Select three to five from this listing to use in the actual vita, or, if requested, during an interview.

Sarah F. Parker 1234 First Avenue Burtonsville, AK 50010-0001

(501) 411-4321 Home (Current address)

Business Address
Riverside College
1420 College Street
College Town, AK 50001-0003

Permanent Address
5678 Lane Street
Lexington, KY 40001-0002
(606) 411-4321

Educational Background

1991   Ph.D. in Political Science, University of Arkansas, Fayetteville, AK
1984   M. A. in Political Science, George Washington University, Washington, DC
1980   B. A. in History, University of Mississippi, Oxford, MS

Other Training
Participated in Workshop for Women in Leadership Positions in Higher Education, sponsored by The American Council on Education, Summer 1980.

Participated in Governmental Affairs Leadership Seminars conducted by American University during the summers of 1981 and 1982 (received certificates of completion).

Governor's School, State of Kentucky, 1975 and 1976

Work Experience

1994-present	Chairperson, Department of Political Science, Riverside College. Coordinate instructional program and research activities. Teach 2-3 courses per semester. Advise both undergraduate and graduate students (master's level).
1987-1994	Associate Professor of Political Science, Riverside College. Taught full-time in department of Political Science. Advised Political Science majors.
1985-1987	Assistant Professor of Political Science and History, University of Arkansas. Full-time teaching in political science and history. Advised undergraduate majors
1980-1983	Administrative Assistant to Congressman Roy Turk. Coordinated office activities including constituent requests and correspondence. Worked with other administrative assistants on problems dealing with legislation and committee assignments of the Congressman. Assisted in drafting legislation.

| 1979-1980 | Research Associate, Governors Task Force on Governmental Affairs, University of Mississippi. Collected data and helped draft report of Task Force to the Governor's Office. |

Part-time Employment

| Summer 1988 | Administrative Assistant to the campaign manager of a congressional election committee. |

| Summer 1980 | Staff Assistant, Governmental Research Center, University of Mississippi. |

Professional Association

American Political Science Association
Organization of American Historians, Southwest Region
American Association of University Professors

Religious Associations

Methodist
Wesley Foundation Advisor, Riverside College

Community Service

Chairperson of Burtonsville, Arkansas Bicentennial Committee, 1992. Served on Governor's Bicentennial Committee for the State of Arkansas, 1991-92.

Foreign Languages

Reading knowledge of French and Spanish

Special Interests

Participation of Women in Politics/Past, Present and Future
Voter Registration
Maximizing Efficiency in Governmental Operations
Political Perspectives on Important Historical Events
Legislative Process

Creative Products

Thesis
Parker, Sarah F. "Political Profiles of Selected Women in American History." Unpublished master's thesis, George Washington University, Washington, DC, 1984.

Dissertation
Parker, Sarah F., "A Political Perspective of the Nineteenth Amendment." Unpublished doctor's thesis, University of Arkansas, 1991.

Publications

Parker, Sarah F., "Women and Politics: A Historical Perspective." American Political Science Review (Bicentennial Issue), 14, 7, 1992.

Parker, Sarah F., "The Struggle for the Vote." American Political Science Review, 14, 3, 1990, pp. 22-32.

Parker, Sarah F., "First Women Officeholders in the South." Tulane Political Quarterly, 58, 1, 1988, pp. 17-24.

Awards and Honors

Alpha Chi Honor Society, University of Mississippi, 1978-1979
Cum Laude Graduate, University of Mississippi, 1980
Forensics Scholarship, University of Mississippi, 1978
Nominee Fullbright Scholarship, 1983

Special Competencies

Teaching
Federal, State, and Local Government
Legislative Process
Voting Behavior
Interest Groups
Public Opinion and Propaganda

Speaking
Women and Voting Rights
Evaluation and Passage of the Nineteenth Amendment
Political Contributions of Women in American History

Have delivered numerous speeches and served on panels at professional meetings.

Also have participated in local, state, and national election campaigns.

Other Work-Related Activities

Served on Editorial Board of the American Political Science Review, 1993

Served on a special committee to study voter registration in the State of Arkansas for the Arkansas State Legislature, 1988.

Served as chairperson of Legislative Liaison Committee, University of Arkansas, 1990

References*

Dr. B. F. Simmons, President
Riverside College
1420 College Street
College Town, AK 50001-0002
(501) 411-2202

Dr. Iris S. Martin, Dean
College of Arts and Sciences
Riverside College
1420 College Street
College Town, AK 50011-0002
(501) 411-2202

The Honorable Roy Turk
Congressman, (Retired)
1010 Grove Street
Lexington, KY 40001-0207
(606) 511-2617

Dr. Jane S. Powell
Department of Political Science
University of Arkansas
Fayetteville, AK 30001-0007
(501) 777-8832

* Additional references are available on request.

January 1996

Vita for William A. Roberts

William A. Roberts

Home Address
1641 Beacon Street
Philadelphia, PA 19123-7774
(215) 321-7654 Voice Mail
(215) 321-7650 Fax

Business Address
Pennsylvania Commission
on Children and Youth
1436 Market Street
Philadelphia, PA 19125-7707
(215) 321-7222

Educational Background

1988	Doctor of Education (Ed. D.) in Educational Administration, University of Pennsylvania, Philadelphia, PA.
1987	Educational Specialist in Education Administration, University of Pennsylvania, Philadelphia, PA.
1984	Master of Arts in Personnel Administration, University of Pennsylvania, Philadelphia, PA.
1979	Bachelor of Arts in Psychology, University of Tennessee, Knoxville, TN.
1975	Diploma, Medford High School, Medford, MI.

Work Experience

1992-present	Executive Director, Pennsylvania Commission on Children and Youth, Philadelphia, PA. Full-time staff director for an agency of 25 professionals. Provide an annual report to the Governor and State Legislature on the work of the Commission. Conduct hearings around the state on topics of current interest to the Commission. Direct staff studies and work with a 20-member commission appointed by the Governor in semi-annual policy meetings.

1988-1992	**Associate Professor of Education, Temple University, Philadelphia, PA. Full-time teacher in the Department of Educational Administration. Assisted in theses development for both master's and doctoral theses committees. Acting chairperson of the Department of Educational Administration 1991-1992. Director of Graduate Research for the Department of Educational Administration, 1990-1992.**
1985-1988	**Principal, Riverview Senior High School, East Bank, PA; Oversaw operation of a senior high school with 2,500 students and 110 staff.**
1983-1985	**Associate Principal, Westside Senior High School, Westside, PA; Assisted principal in the operation of a senior high school with 1,800 students and a staff of 85. Coached varsity golf team.**
1981-1983	**Teacher, Westside Senior High School, Westside, PA; Taught social studies at grades 10, 11 and 12; Served as faculty sponsor for the Student Government Association; Coached varsity golf team.**

Part-time

Winter 1987	**Administrative intern with the Superintendent of Philadelphia's Public School System; Major responsibility to update the System's Faculty Handbook; Also helped plan citywide conference of educational administrators and assisted the Superintendent with other special projects.**
1985-1987	**Taught extension courses for Temple University (in Philadelphia) in the area of educational administration and secondary school curriculum.**
Summer 1984	**Worked in the City Recreation Department for the City of Tallahassee, FL.**
Summer 1981	**Directed community recreation program in Westside, PA for secondary school students.**

Summer 1980   Directed community recreation program in
               Westside, PA for elementary school students.

Summer 1977   Employed by the Recreation Department City of Summer
1978 Knoxville, TN.

Memberships in Professional Associations and Offices Held

National Mental Health Association, Current
National Education Association, Current
Pennsylvania Education Association, Current
Vice-President of the Pennsylvania Education Association, 1987
Philadelphia Education Society, Current
President, Philadelphia Educational Society, 1986
Phi Delta Kappa, Current
National Association of Elementary and Secondary School Principals,
    Current
Candidate for President, Pennsylvania Association of Elementary and
    Secondary School Principals, 1991

Religious Affiliations and Activities

Member of the First Baptist Church of Philadelphia; Teach Young Adults
Bible Class; Men's Choir; Served as Church Treasurer for two years.

Community Service Activities

Manned phone for Philadelphia Area March of Dimes Telethon, 1987-90.
Volunteer worker for the American Cancer Society, 1989-92; Coordinated
three Red Cross Blood Mobile Drives for the City of Westside, PA 1979-82.

Leisure Activities

Golf, tennis, bowling, swimming, and reading.

Foreign Languages

Reading knowledge of French.

Military Experiences

Branch of Service: U. S. Navy - 1979-1981

Military Experiences Continued

Highest Rank Attained: Lieutenant (Junior Grade)

Worked as communications officer on destroyers and an
aircraft carriers.

Special Research Interests

Prevention of Child Abuse
Competency-based administrator training
Secondary School curriculum
Community Education

Creative Products

Publications

Roberts, William A., "Future Trends in Educational Administration."
Education Magazine, Vol. 10, no. 2, October 1993, 20-17.

Roberts, William A., "Toward Competency-Based Administrator
Training." Journal of Educational Administration, Vol. 9, No.   4, December
1992, 17-78.

Roberts, William A., "The Right Thing To Do: Discipline in the Secondary
School Setting." Education Magazine, Vol. 8,   No. 6, February 1991, 14-
28.

Roberts, William A., "Principle or Principal." Secondary School
Administrator, Vol. 2, No. 2, Winter, 1990, 41-48.

Roberts, William A., "Staff Development in the Secondary School."
       Secondary School Administrator, Vol. 1, No. 4, Summer, 1989, 19-24.

Roberts, William A., "Community Education: Articulation or Bust."
       Community Education Review, Vol. 3, No. 5, February 1988,   32-37.

Roberts, William A., "Politics and the Principal." Pennsylvania Education
Association Newsletter, Spring 1988, 2-3.

Roberts, William A., "Perceptions of the Secondary School Principal's Role
in the Evaluation of Faculty Classroom Performance." Unpublished
doctoral dissertation, The University of Pennsylvania, 1988.

Papers Presented at Professional Meetings

"Future Trends in Educational Administration." Paper presented at the University of Pennsylvania Symposium on Education, Philadelphia, January 12, 1992.

"Secondary School Staff Development." Paper presented at the National Association of Elementary and Secondary School Administrators Conference, Houston, Texas, March 12-15, 1991.

"Community Education and the Secondary School Principal." Paper presented at the National Association of Elementary and Secondary School Administrators Annual Meeting, Atlanta, GA, March 10-13, 1987.

"Does it Hurt Us More Than Them: Discipline in the Public Schools." Paper presented at the National Education Association Annual Meetings, St. Louis, MI, June 14-18, 1986.

Research Proposals Written and Funded

U. S. Department of Education proposal funded at $57,000 (July 1, 1991 to June 30, 1992), to prepare a Staff Development Model for the Pennsylvania Public Schools.

National Education Association grant funded at $20,000 (July 1, 1990 through December 31, 1990), to report on the impact of the community education concept in the State of Pennsylvania.

U. S. Department of Education proposal funded at $51,000 (July 1, 1989 through June 30, 1990), to study discipline problems in Pennsylvania Public Schools.

Awards and Honors

1988 Distinguished Service Award, Riverview High School P. T. A.

Awards and Honors Continued

1987 Leadership Award, Pennsylvania Education Association
1985 Outstanding Young Educator, City of Philadelphia
1984 Coach of the Year, Westside Senior High School,
     Westside, PA

Special Competencies

University Courses Taught

Theories of Educational Administration
Curriculum Development in the Secondary School
Supervision of Instruction in the Secondary School
Personnel Administration
Community Relations Seminar
School Law

Committee Work

Governor's Task Force on Cost Reduction in Pennsylvania State Government, 1992-1993.

Temple University, College of Education, Curriculum Evaluation Committee; 1990-1991, Revised College of Education Faculty Handbook.

Temple University, College of Education, Faculty Evaluation Committee; 1989-1990, worked on the comprehensive revision of the faculty evaluation program for the College of Education.

Pennsylvania Education Association, Nominations Committee; Chairperson 1989-1990, in charge of selecting nominees for the year beginning July, 1, 1990.

National Association of Secondary School Principals, Program Committee, Chairperson, 1989-1990; Coordinated planning for the Association's annual meeting.

Certification Status

Class A Teaching Certificate for the State of Pennsylvania--1981
Class A Principal's Certificate for the State of Pennsylvania--1983

Class A Superintendent's Certificate for the State of Pennsylvania--1985
CAE (Certified Association Executive), issued by the National Conference of Association Executives--1993.

Other Work-Related Activities

Consulting

Pittsburgh, Pennsylvania City School System, led Staff Development
Workshop, June 12-17, 1993.

Wichita, Kansas, led Community Education Workshop,
November 2-4, 1992.

Harrisburg, Pennsylvania Public Schools, led Staff Development
Workshop, August 15-19, 1991.

Cleveland, Ohio, staff member of Community Education Workshop,
July 15-18, 1990.

Gettysburg County Schools, Pennsylvania, led Staff Development
Workshop, August 1-4, 1989.

U. S. Department of Education, Washington, D. C., member Task Force on
Discipline in the Secondary School, Summer, 1988.

References

Dr. Marie D. Fredericks
Dean, College of Education
Temple University
Philadelphia, PA 19125-0021
(215) 321-7111

Dr. William B. Wilson
Chairperson, Department of Educational Administration
Temple University
Philadelphia, PA 19125-0021
(215) 321-7014

The two sample vitas provide examples of how individual candidates may emphasize important items or highlight strengths likely to be of interest to employers and colleagues in their fields.

The vita for Sarah F. Parker cites numerous examples of her involvement in research, writing, political activities, and women's issues--all important as a part of her qualifications for teaching and administering political science activities.

The vita for William A. Roberts is filled with content about teaching and other jobs in education, both during the school year and through summer recreation department jobs. These are well supported by memberships and offices in professional education associations. As in the case of Sarah Parker, no space is devoted to family and personal matters.

These are both general vitas. If one of them were applying for a particular position, there could be a special highlights section on the individual's special strengths. The highlighted sections, such as in the following example, provide the vita reader with a quick look and serves to entice them into reading further.

William A. Roberts
Vita Highlights

For the past 25 years I have been active in teaching, coaching, and educational administration in public schools, higher education, and state-level agency settings. Accomplishments include leadership assignments in a variety of educational, community, and professional association activities.

Chapter 6

Revising and Finalizing the Vita

If you have followed the suggestions already offered in this book, the most difficult parts of developing your vita are over. This chapter seeks to help you make a good product even better. If you do not have a good foundation by now--revising and finalizing are not going to help much. Perhaps the most important task after getting all of your worksheets in order and a strong draft that is ready to send out. Follow the suggestion about obtaining <u>three critical readers</u> of your final draft. This feedback is crucial in preparing to review and finalize your vita. Before you begin this stage, review the six key points, brought out in earlier chapters, as a checklist to confirm your correctness.

1.   Conceptualize

Be sure you know how you want to use the vita.

Be sure it presents your best image.

Be sure it is written to be understood by readers who do not know you.

2.   Complete

Be sure worksheets contain complete and current information.

Be sure you have pulled all of the key information for your special
       purpose from the professional summaries worksheets.

Be sure you have included important professional portfolio data in
       your draft.

3.   Clear

Be sure a sound and easily understood organizational plan is followed

Be sure there is no confusion concerning any entry.

Be sure it is readable.

4.   Concise

Be sure it is not too long.

Be sure it is not padded.

Be sure there are no double enteries.

5.   Consistent

Be sure it does not mix styles.

Be sure all sequences are in proper order.

Be sure there is an appearance of evenness.

6.   Current

Be sure there are no out-of-date entries.

Be sure there is a date at the beginning or the end.

Be sure activities from recent months are included.

In addition to the above list, two other general points may help to put your mind at ease when you are debating whether or not to include an item. First, there is no perfect vita format. You could read 100 vitaes, all good, and decide that each one has some special strength--yet, each is unique. These are general guidelines to follow, but so many options exist that you are ultimately going to have to pick a format based on the purpose you want your vita to serve, and how best to present the information..

Second, no matter how many vitas you have studied, you are going to have to select what goes in yours based on <u>your best judgment and your good taste</u>. <u>There is no substitute for these two</u>. However, these suggestions are difficult to illustrate or teach--but there are several ways to attempt to develop some sensitivity in this area. One is to ask a co-worker who has a good vita, good judgment, or both to review your final draft copy. Another is to ask to review the vita of an active professional person whom colleagues have told you has an outstanding vita, for ideas. Chances are, the individual will be flattered by your attention and share the vita with you.

A final suggestion is to volunteer for committees that review vitaes. In addition to your own observations, you might ask committee members with whom you serve to comment on the strengths and weaknesses of the materials they are reviewing, especially where they see good judgment and taste and where they see poor judgment and poor taste. These suggestions, along with the useful comments of your critic readers, should form the basis for a solid professional vita.

Vita Preparation and Reproduction

This may appear to be a minor clerical matter, but you can spend hours gathering all available data, putting it together properly, revising and editing suggestions, review by critic readers--then have a poor preparation or poor duplication effort spoil the entire professional look you are trying to achieve. Start with these five negatives:

- Do not use sloppy copy.

- Do not use cheap duplication processes.
- Do not use wild color paper.
- Do not use cheap paper.
- Do not use dot-matrix printers.

Follow these five positives:

- Do insist on an attractive layout.
- Do use high quality computer generated print that is easy to read.
- Do utilize a skilled keyboard professional look.
- Do use a high-quality light paper. (white, ivory, buff, etc.)
- Do use a high-quality duplication process.

To implement these suggestions, start with quality keyboarding from easy-too use graphic and word processing programs. Use the best quality 8 1/2" x 11" size plain bond paper. The presentation must be perfect. This is an absolute must. There must be no errors.

It should be carefully proofread by at least two other people to be absolutely sure there are no errors. The layout must be uniform throughout, with 1 1/4" or 1 1/2" margins all around. There are a variety of typefaces available to choose from using various word processing programs. Just be sure the size of type will produce a professional product. If you use a typewriter, be sure your ribbon is new for the best impressions.

Once you have a perfect copy, what printers refer to as "camera ready copy," look for a local print shop or photocopy center that can take your materials and reproduce them through a process that will provide a clear, high-quality finished product. The outcome of this process should be a professionally printed vita. The cost of this will vary in different parts of the country for a five-page printed vita on good quality paper. The cost should be about $5.00 for ten copies.

The process above is suggested for anything over 10 copies. If you need fewer copies for a special purpose, such as presenting yourself for membership in a professional organization, then use some type of standard office copy method, such as photocopying. Just insist on quality copies that come out clear with no dark borders, streaks, blurs, or blots. Whatever method of duplication you use, a single staple in the upper left-hand corner is adequate for holding the pages together.

If you want an especially fancy job done, you may ask a print shop to cite prices on professional type set or computer generated composition. This means the printer may use several styles to highlight headings, special entries, or different categories. The cost for this may be $10 to $25 per page. Also, be prepared to wait a few days for composition setting. Once this is complete you will still need a good quality duplication process to complement the more expensive composition type. Copy centers such as Kinko's can usually perform this service for you.

If you have access to a personal computer and a good laser jet printer-- then you may choose to produce your vita on an as-needed basis, and make only a few copies at a time. This also will allow you to customize your vita for each special purpose.

Chapter 7

Developing the Resume

With the completed professional portfolio worksheets available and your vita as a guide, <u>developing your resume should be easy</u>. Both documents have their roots in the worksheets. So go back and review the information you have put down on the worksheets. Be sure of the items and that the information is complete and up to date.

First, decide how you want to use your resume. Conceptualize your use. Second, since the resume is much shorter than the vita, you can more easily develop a number of versions depending upon its use, with a variety of formats. Do not make the mistake of thinking that resumes are just used for job hunting, or can only be assembled in one way--both ideas are wrong.

The best way to approach the resume is to develop one that can be used for general purposes. One that you could safely send to a local Rotary Club or anywhere you have been invited to speak. Another use of a general resume is to accompany a program proposal or for a committee charged with reviewing applications for a highly competitive training workshop. In short, there are likely to be a number of uses for a general resume in the course of a year. If you revise your professional summary each January, you can simply make the necessary modifications and reorganize your resume to fit a specific use--using a preliminary job announcement in the same manner you would prior to sending out your vita for job-hunting purposes.

Most professionals find that a strong general resume and a convincing cover letter can serve many needs throughout the year. Of course, if you are job hunting you will want to target your cover letter, vita or resume to suit that specific purpose and--one size does not fit all purposes.

Using the Resume

The resume should be used for specific situations where general, not detailed, information is needed. It can be used for many of the same purposes as the vita--but where less detail seems appropriate. Both can be used for introductions. A resume may suffice for most occasions, while a vita might be more appropriate for a national professional meeting. Likewise a resume may be useful for wide circulation when you are looking for a job in a broad geographical area and with a large number of potential employees. It can be used to explore and locate potential employees. If, however, you are responding to a known vacancy, where a detailed citation of your background is requested, then by all means, send your tailor-made vita and a carefully written cover letter.

Resume Contents

The content of the resume will depend almost entirely on its purpose and format. However, certain key items will appear in almost all resumes. In using information from your worksheets, you should observe the following principals:

1. You must <u>try</u> to keep it to one page.
2. You must get the reader's attention quickly.
3. You must make the organization clear.
4. You must make it attractive.
5. You must include key contact information.
6. You must use bold, eye-catching graphics.
7. You must leave plenty of open space.

8. You must keep it balanced.

9. You may need to alter it for competitive scanning, if called for.

10. You must include a current year's date--

Fall 1996 or January 1, 1996, or the date of your cover letter--

make the date on your resume a clear point of currentness.

Most people agree with points 2-9. Over the years people have taken issue with points 1 and 10, which, from the standpoint of this book, are strongly encouraged. The ultimate choice on all of the items in this book or any other of the dozens available, is up to you. The reader dictates how you want your vita or resume to look. Take all of this or any other book as offering lots of suggestions and encouragement. You are the ultimate person in charge of your vita and resume. So the question for point No. 1 is: "Can you keep your resume to one page?" The answer is clearly YES. Everybody can summarize, prioritize, and highlight their professional background on one page. This is referred to in this book as the one-page general resume. Everybody can produce a general one-page resume. Not everybody wants to cut their professional background down to one page--so make it two, three, or even four pages. Some employers are, in fact, asking for longer resumes with very specific identification of duties and responsibilities in previous work settings as well as requested descriptions of competencies and skills. There are occasions when, to meet employer requests or your need to more fully describe your professional background, you may feel you need two or three pages--you decide. Remember that most readers will spend, by most estimates, less than 120 seconds reviewing a resume. For a job application, many estimates suggest reviewers spend around 30 to 60 seconds or less.

On the matter of point No. 10, including a date on your resume, the same principle applies: You decide. This book suggests you include a date on your vita or resume.

Why should you include a date?

- It shows that you care about keeping your resume current.

- It shows that you want the reader to know it is current.

- It shows that you do not want to be considered out-of-date.

- It shows that you care how your resume looks.

- It shows your resume is current, and the date proves it.

Now if you feel there are some good solid reasons to leave the date off-- leave it off. Weigh the pros and cons and you decide.

Key Considerations

Personal Contact Information- The same kind of information which appears in the vita can be used here. A full listing of your name, address, phone number, voice mail information, if available, and fax number is essential for easy communication with readers. In most cases it is best to keep this at the top where it is easy to find and read. To save space, you can put your home address and phone number by the left margin and your work address and phone number by the right margin. If in doubt, leave it out.

Education Background- This should be a very brief listing of your degrees, institutions, (and location) major fields and dates. Start with your most recent degree, if you have more than one. Normally you would not show short-term education or training experiences in the limited space available in a resume. If there are particularly appropriate special kinds of schools or programs you have attended, go ahead and summarize them--but briefly, and only if space is available.

Employment History- Again, this can parallel the data used in the vita. The main difference is that this section will contain only the highlights--showing job title, employer and address, and dates of employment, for the most part. Furthermore, unless you have a very brief work history, you will probably want to show full-time work only. If you feel it will strengthen your resume to list part-time, summer, or volunteer work (especially full-time work like Ameri- Corps) go ahead and do so, but only if space permits. Military service activity, if any, should be included under this heading.

Professional Association Activities- A list of current memberships, along with important key elected or appointed positions, may be reported here. Significant honors and awards of a professional association nature can be shown here as well.

Leisure Activities- If space permits and if they are related to your objective in using the resume, you may refer to significant leisure activities in this section. Clearly, you want to avoid being trite or boastful. For example, if you are a competitive long distance runner or a champion chess player, that might be cited to show something of what you are like--rather than harping upon your victories and trophies. Once again use good taste and judgment.

Creative Activities- A summary of principle activities may be all that space will permit, so you might want to use a narrative approach (rather than a detailed listing) such as "published articles in ..." or "exhibits of paintings held in..." or "patents held on the following items..."

Special Heading- There are, of course, a variety of other topics which could be included in your resume, if space permits. You may, for example, be very active in civic, religious, or service organizations with important posts held over a period of years. If so, it may be appropriate to have a special entry for two to three such items. Also, there may be a significant record of participation or accomplishments in dramatics, athletics, or volunteer work which you want to report. You can vary main categories on the resume or combine them depending upon what information you feel should be emphasized for general or specific purposes.

Items on Request- A resume generally does not include references. However, you might indicate that references are available upon request. <u>If you are using the resume for job hunting purposes</u> only you may want to indicate that a vita is also available upon request. Obviously you do not list references on your resume for an introduction at the local Rotary Club. You might consider preparing a separate reference listing and have it available to include in any application packet.

Pictures- For a variety of reasons, this is a very sensitive matter. No employer or user of your resume can request that a picture be included unless it fulfills a bona fide occupational requirement, so the option of submitting a picture is totally yours. This is usually reserved for dramatic and modeling occupations. However, after you are hired, the employer may ask for a photograph to put in your personnel file, to be used on your identification badge, etc..

Draft Review- You have a number of options for assembling your resume. The best procedure is to develop a rough draft under four to six main headings and see what style is most appropriate for your general purposes. When you have developed your final draft, have it reviewed by several critic readers (see Chapter 5). With their comments at hand, you should be ready to develop your final copy. Use the suggestions for preparation and duplication described in Chapter 6.

Updating- <u>Every resume should be updated at least annually</u>. There may be reasons why you would want to update sooner, such as a change in address, promotion, or a significant book or article published, etc. The best time to do this is in January--then it will timely for the next 12 months. There are no good reasons for using an out-of-date resume.

Special Job Hunting Information- Some people feel that a resume that is being used for job-hunting purposes should state the kind or type of position sought, even the salary level you expect. Again, this is strictly a matter of taste and judgment. If the resume is used to respond to a specific job announcement, it hardly seems necessary to state what kind of job you want. On the other hand, if you expect to send your resume out to a large number of employers on your own initiative, including your position preferences, it probably makes sense. The same holds true for salary information: include it only if you expect to use the resume widely, with a large number of potential employers who might not know what salary suits you. Otherwise, leave it out. Likewise, creating a special heading on a job-hunting resume as to when you are available to begin work may be wise in this section. You might state, <u>"Available to start work July 1, 1997"</u>, if you expect to complete a degree in June 1997.

Headings and Layout- The use of headings and layout are especially important to your resume. Since it is short, you have to communicate with a quick feeling of clear, concise, confident appearance at first glance. Depending upon the length of your material, you may want to use either the center heads or left margin heads. You may want to use all capital letters of a different type style in the headings. In a recent study, it was found that employers wanted a resume with distinct headings, clear organization, and an attractive, uncluttered format. See Chapter 9 on electronic resumes for special instruction in that area. For your general resume, use the headings and layout that you think looks best.

Use at least double spacing between each section and provide at least 1"-1 1/4" to 1"-1 1/2" margins at the top and bottom as well as the left and right margins. Plenty of "open space" will make your resume more attractive to the reader. Some employers like to have wide margins for making notes.

Also, consider overall balance and appearance in developing your resume. If you are beginning full-time work and your resume is running a bit short, feel free to use some sections that you might not otherwise consider, or spread out the data with some extra open space on the page at the top and bottom. For young workers, employers urge students to add honors, achievements, and extracurricular activities. Try for balance between the various sections, so that some don't look too long and others inappropriately short. The mature worker who has been through a long work history will have to exercise the same good judgment at the opposite extreme to avoid a cluttered look.

Hint: If you are having difficulty getting all of what you think is vita information on your one-page resume, remember you can use a smaller type style or reduce the copy to fit on an 8 1/2" x 11" sheet of paper.

Types of Resume Styles

Chronological- the chronological resume is designed to provide a comprehensive summary of all major educational and employment experience. All employment experiences, even those not relevant to the position being sought, are cited. Resumes of William White and Sarah Parker, which follow, illustrate the chronological style.

Functional - The functional resume is designed to emphasize work experiences, important skills, or other significant accomplishments, and is frequently used by individuals who have held a variety of positions. The functional format can be used effectively to minimize a record of frequent job changes. The examples of Linda Arnold and David Smith show functional resumes.

There are many ways a resume can be assembled. You can use some very creative approaches to try and attract attention or to emphasize certain points. The chronological style represents the most common format for general purpose uses as well as for job hunting. Employers seem to favor the chronological style. The functional style is used almost exclusively for job hunting purposes. You should not feel limited by the guidelines suggested or the samples shown. Review them to observe a variety of styles, principles, approaches, and combinations of information which you can modify to suit your own needs. Take some time to develop several resumes that you feel best reflects your achievements and accomplishments.

Computer Graphic Software Packages

There are a number of commercial or inexpensive resume computer graphics software packages available. Just be sure these services can produce a better resume than you can on your own using this book and other sources. Once you tie into any one of these programs, you usually have to follow the instructions provided. If you do your own work, you can modify it any way you like.

Sarah F. Parker 1234 First Avenue Burtonsville, AK 50010-0001

(501) 411-4321 Home (Current address)

Business Address
Riverside College
1420 College Street
College Town, AK 50001-0003

Permanent Address
5678 Lane Street
Lexington, KY 40001-0002
(606) 411-4321

Educational Background

1991	Ph.D. in Political Science, University of Arkansas, Fayetteville, AK
1984	M. A. in Political Science, George Washington University, Washington, DC
1980	B. A. in History, University of Mississippi, Oxford, MS

Other Training
Participated in Workshop for Women in Leadership Positions in Higher Education, sponsored by The American Council on Education, Summer 1980.

Work History

1991-Present	Chairperson, Department of Political Science, Riverside College, College Town, AK.
1984-1991	Assistant Professor of Political Science and History, College of Ft. Smith, Ft. Smith, AK.
1980-1984	Administrative Assistant to Congressman W.F. Turk, U. S. House of Representatives, Washington, D. C.
1979-1980	Research Associate, Governor's Task Force on Governmental Affairs, Jackson, MS.
Note: 1986-1987	Part-time Faculty Member at the College of Ft. Smith, AK and a graduate student at the University of Arkansas.

Professional Associations

American Political Science Association
Organization of American Historians, Southwest Region
American Association of University Professors

Awards and Honors

Alpha Chi Honor Society, University of Mississippi, 1978-1979
Cum Laude Graduate, University of Mississippi, 1980
Forensics Scholarship, University of Mississippi, 1978
Nominee Fullbright Scholarship, 1983

September 1996

WILLIAM WHITE
262 Cascade Avenue
Bering, OK 71601-7654
(320) 471-2215 voice mail

EMPLOYMENT BACKGROUND
1987-present   **Budget Officer, Central State College,**
                                    Bering, OK; Coordinated fiscal activities and
                                    developed annual budget for an institution
with a cash flow of $50,000 per year.

1985-1987   **Established automated accounting system in**
                                    the largest bank in the community.

1981-1985   **Accountant, self-employed, Ames, IA;**
                                    Handled accounts for a variety of business
                                    and social service agencies while attending
                                    Iowa State University as a part-time student.

1978-1981   **Auditor, Sears and Roebuck Company;**
                                    Checked on accounting procedures at 20
                                    stores in a five-state area.

OTHER EMPLOYMENT
Salesman in retail food and clothing store while attending high school and
college; Kept financial records for father's hardware business; Completed
tax returns for relatives and friends.

PROFESSIONAL AND CIVIC ASSOCIATIONS
Kiwanis Club of Bering, OK (served as club treasurer for five years)
American Association of Certified Public Accountants (served as
association contact for the State of Oklahoma for three years)
Oklahoma Association of Collegiate Financial Officers (served as president
1994-1995)

EDUCATION
1985 Passed Certified Public Accountant Examination in October
1983 MBA, Iowa State University, Ames Iowa
1978 BA, Business Administration University of Oklahoma Norman, OK

October 1996

Linda F. Arnold 1977 Lake Drive, Norfolk, VA 22222-0202
(804) 791-3524   larn@norfolk.infi.net

COMPETENCIES

Coaching Experience- Two years as head coach of 8th and 9th grade women's basketball; Three years as head coach of 10th grade women's basketball and assistant coach of women's varsity basketball; Five years as head coach of women's varsity basketball; Eight years as head coach of women's varsity track team.

Playing Experience- Four-year starter for the women's basketball team at Hampton University and in high school; Sprinter and long jumper in college; Also active in tennis, golf, and rowing.

Teaching Experience- Taught physical education, family life education, and first aid courses at the junior high school level for two years. Taught physical education and American history at the senior high school level for eight years.

Community Service- Coordinated women's basketball league for YWCA for five years; Directed personal hygiene seminars for teenage boys and girls in Upward Bound Program; Gave health tips seminar for senior citizen's club; Served as consultant at the local and state levels as judge for Virginia's Special Olympics Program.

PROFESSIONAL ASSOCIATIONS

Active member for 15 years in the Virginia Education Association serving as building representative. County president and state delegate (served 10 years). Officer and committee chair in the local, state, and National Association of Coaches.

EDUCATION

1986   Master of Science in Physical Education, Virginia State College, Petersburg, VA

1984   Bachelor of Science in Physical Education, Hampton   University, Hampton, VA

1984   Hold permanent teaching certificate in Virginia

June 1996

David K. Smith
3456 East Pine Street
Turnerville, Texas 78789-0708
(200) 612-4500

JOB OBJECTIVE

Experienced vocational educator seeks leadership position with a growing community college. Prefer an administrative position with the opportunity for occasional part-time teaching.

EMPLOYMENT

Administration-- Served as chairperson for occupational education section of junior college for two years. Held office as vice-president of state vocational education association, with responsibility for membership and finances for a three-year term. Served on numerous church and civic committees concerned with management activities.

Teaching-- Taught in three high schools in southwestern Texas including courses in industrial arts, vocational education, and driver education. Served as part-time adult education teacher for two years. Taught several courses while serving as a junior college administrator.

Practical Work in the Field-- Employed as an industrial engineer in manufacturing firm for one year. Worked four summers in construction fields during the period of undergraduate and graduate training.

EDUCATION

Master of Arts in Industrial Education, Texas A & M University, College Station TX, 1986

Bachelor of Science in Industrial Education in Engineering, Texas A & M University, College Station TX, 1981

Associate of Applied Science, Houston Technical Institute, Houston, TX, 1979

AWARDS AND HONORS

1975 Outstanding Senior, Industrial Engineering, Texas A & M University, 1981
Employee of the Year, Fullerton Industries, 1983
Honors Award for Research in Industrial Education, Texas A & M University, 1985

Availability-- 30 Days Notice   References-- Available Upon Request
July 1996

Chapter 8

Covering the Cover Letter

Since the first edition of this book was published, the importance of the cover letter has grown in significance. The simple reason is that jobs at almost every level have become more competitive. Next to your own vita or resume, the cover letter is the most crucial way to make an impression. A cover letter that carries an impact can get a more careful look at your vita or resume. Do not underestimate the power of the cover letter when applying for a job or when describing to your current employer the highlights of your work over the last year.

Here are some common-sense suggestions for producing a quality cover letter:

Style

- <u>Always keep your cover letter to one page</u> with wide margins and block-style heading for an even look. Of   course, make sure it is well prepared and error free printed on high quality white, ivory, or buff paper.

- Keep your cover letter brief and to the point. <u>Never</u> write more than four or five short paragraphs.

- Make sure you have the correct spelling, name, title, and address of the person to whom you are sending the letter.

- Make sure you list the same address that is on your vita or resume. Also, be sure the address is current and can receive express delivery service.

- Be sure to sign your letter. A surprisingly high percentage of application letters fail to carry a signature, and this carelessness sends them directly to the wastebasket

Content

- Introduce your reason for applying in the first paragraph for the job or a promotion. Make a clear, interesting case for why you are presenting yourself in the first place. If you get the reader's attention, your resume and letter will get further consideration. Do not make it sound like a mass mailing.

- The second paragraph should clearly explain why you feel qualified for the position under consideration. Point out 1-2-3 reasons in clear, direct language using action verbs. Connect this paragraph to the job announcement. Use similar words and emphasize why you are worth a   more careful look.

- Follow up in the third paragraph with some unique skills and accomplishments that might make you stand out from other people, such as a recent paper published or an award you received. If you are applying for a university teaching position, offer to send a sample one-hour videotaped class multi-media presentation.

- Close by indicating your interest in the position and that you will follow up by letter or telephone to confirm receipt of your materials and, hopefully, schedule an interview. You may want to offer to provide a sample of your writing or future information, if useful. Make it a strong, forceful, interesting closing paragraph.

If you are just forwarding your vita or resume for purposes of an introduction at a professional presentation or some other potential presentation, you may simply state your reason for the letter, refer to the enclosure, and mention your willingness to provide further information if that would be helpful.

What follows are three sample letters for very different situations. Stick with understanding the principle stated above and get an idea of the look and style in the sample. You have to make a personal connection between you and the person to whom you are writing. Fifty or even one hundred examples will not do that unless you follow some simple guidelines.

At the end of the chapter is an Employer Contact Log to use in recording job search activities and to help coordinate your follow-up efforts.

Sample Cover Letter 1

1040 North Shore Drive
Chicago, IL 6007-0303
January 4, 1996

Mr. Gene Donaldson
Personnel Manager
Westsouth Dam Company
4723 East Front Street
Portland, OR

Dear Mr. Donaldson:

This is in response to your advertisement for an electrical engineer in the Engineering Placement Quarterly of December 1995. My background and experience appear to coincide with your position, since I have had four years of industrial supervisory responsibility in tool production.

As you will note from the attached vita, I am familiar with the Oregon area. I grew up in Portland, attended Oregon State University, and worked two years for the Bonneville Dam Authority before accepting my present job in Chicago. I took this position to learn as much as possible about management, through actual work with one of the best-run companies in the business. Now I am ready to return to Oregon and your position seems ideal.

At the present time, I am being considered for promotion with my current organization. If a job is contemplated, out of fairness to my present employer, it would be best to know that as soon as possible.

I plan to be in the Portland area on vacation in approximately two weeks and would welcome a chance to talk with you at that time.

Please let me know if additional information would be of use to you. I look forward to hearing from you.

Sincerely Yours,

Harry Jones

Encl.

Sample Cover Letter-2

732 Longhorn Drive
Austin, TX
July 1, 1996

Dr. June Appleton, Dean
College of Arts and Sciences
Bayview University
Key West, FL 36247-0007

Dear Dean Appleton:

I have read about your vacancy for an Assistant Professor of Chemistry in the June 20, 1996 issue of the <u>Chronicle of Higher Education</u>. As requested in the notice of vacancy, a copy of my vita is enclosed. My dissertation has been accepted and I expect to receive my Ph. D. degree on August 15. It would be possible to come for an interview at any time before then.

As you will note in my vita, I have had ten years of industrial experience in research and development work. Our mutual friend, Dr. Lisa Wright, has agreed to write you concerning my qualifications. While I might go back to industry, my goal in returning to graduate school was to enter college teaching, but my main objective now is to develop into a top-flight instructor.

My credentials are being sent directly to you by the placement office here at the University of Texas.

Several other institutions have expressed interest in my qualifications, possibly because I have both industrial experience and recent graduate work in chemistry. For this reason, an early indication of your interest would be appreciated. As I grew up in southern Florida and would like to begin my teaching career in a smaller institution, Bayview University is of particular interest to me.

Your serious consideration of my qualifications will be much appreciated. Please let me know if additional information would be useful.

Sincerely yours,

Doris Smith

Encl.

Sample Cover Letter-3

17 "Z" Street N. W.
Washington, D. C.
October 15, 1996

Ms. Jane Zephart
Personnel Director
District of Columbia
District Building
141 Indiana Avenue, N. W.
Washington D. C. 20001-0101

Dear Ms. Zephart:

Sue Zimmerman, the Women's Action Coordinator in the Office of the Mayor, has called to my attention the vacancy for an Administrative Assistant in the Office of Human Development. This sounds exactly like the kind of position I have been looking for elsewhere.

As you will note on the attached resume, I have a B. S. degree in psychology and special training in public administration. For several years, I worked as an administrative assistant for a Congressman. I dropped out of the labor market for 10 years to raise a family and now am available for full-time employment.

During this 10-year period, I have kept active through participation in a number of volunteer and part-time activities. I have served as an election poll watcher for my district, worked in the legislative review committee of the D. C. League of Women Voters, and handled all hiring for the past five years for Camp Goodwill. As you know, Camp Goodwill is sponsored by the Agency for Social Concern and I was its Personnel Committee Chairperson.

I will call your office next week to see if an appointment can be arranged. Thank you in advance for reviewing my qualifications.

Very truly yours,

Mary S. Moore

Encl.

Employer Contact Log

	Sent To	Date Sent	Response	Follow-up	Comment
1.					
2.					
3.					
4.					
5.					
6.					
7.					
8.					
9.					
10.					

Chapter 9

Producing an Electronic Resume

Many resumes today are no longer personally scrutinized by a personnel worker who is puts them into two piles: reject and possible. Instead, more and more organizations scan resumes using computers eliminating many because they fail to use key words--the same words cited in the job announcement.

Optical character recognition (OCR) software scans resumes and creates a file that may be "read" to abstract basic information (name, address, education, etc.) and to pick up the key words that describe the kinds of experience an applicant has. Therefore, unless your resume contains the same key words that appear in the description of vacancies in an organization, you will not receive consideration.

To make sure that electronic reading of their resumes is an asset rather than a liability, candidates often put a "Key Words Summary" right at the top where career objective used to appear. Think about how an employer describes a job. For example, if you have been a teacher in a school system but would like to end up as a corporate trainer, then use a word like "training" to describe your recent work.

As a recent article in the <u>National Business Employment Weekly</u> pointed out, you might want to submit your qualifications two ways: one faxed or e-mailed resume, which you assume will be computer scanned, and a conventional letter of application and resume that gives the employer a clearer sense of the kind of person you are. This seems a sensible suggestion.

So what may have been only dreamed about 5-10-15 years ago is beginning to emerge as a legitimate way of sending or transmitting your resume. The content, clarity, consistency, and conciseness of the information discussed earlier in this book is still the same. The big difference here is (1) how you may be required to put this information together and (2) how you send it and (3) what employers do with your resume when they receive it. More and more they scan it into a computer. Both of these changes are significant in how and why you create your resume and what happens to it.

This book is addressed to the professional reader who most likely has at least a master's degree, first professional or doctorate and is looking for a position in some type of higher education institution or a related professional association, public or private agency, or related setting. Most opportunities in this area are listed in the Chronicle of Higher Education. Employers often request the following three things from candidates:

1. A cover letter- Chapter 8

2. A resume or vita- Chapter 6 and 7

3. A list of three to six references- Chapter 4

There are occasional requests for some type of electronic transmittal, but for now the procedures in this book should prepare you for a careful consideration no matter what employers want.

Likewise, if you are contacted after a professional conference presentation by someone who liked your research or presentation, they are most likely to ask for a printed copy of your resume/vita or request that you send one with a cover letter. Young professionals may want to have a resume with them at such presentations.

Employers who are not in higher education may ask for something quite different. For example, the largest school district in Virginia has gone to a "no-application-resume-only system." The resume is requested by fax, even though it will be accepted with a cover letter. It is prescribed in a very precise form by the employer, not necessarily in the resume writer's format as described in this book. Since 1995, the same is true of the federal government. No longer does an applicant fill out a rigid S-F 171 form. Now one follows a more flexible plan as described by the Office of Personnel Management in the Guidelines for Applying for a Federal Job 0F510.

Similarly, if you are searching for a job with one of the many on-line computer job search sites, you may be asked to respond with an electronic resume and cover letter. It is estimated that the listing of such services is now over 200 and growing. The most comphrensive, America's Job Bank, http://www.ajb.dni.us/ which has over 500,000 job listings and had seven million users in July 1996. This service is sponsored by the U. S. Department of Labor and carries job listings by large and small employers from all over the United States. Along the same direction is a computer software system called Resume Expert Plus (RE+) which is being used in over 250 colleges and universities around the country. This system structures your resume to fit the electronic network and provides several resume styles with a number of format options that in turn can be used for a wide variety of purposes. There are other computer software systems like Resume Expert Plus.

What Should You Do?

Clearly the well-prepared professional needs to be <u>ready</u> for both conventional print and electronic options for vitas and resumes. This book should have provided you with the framework to do just that by completing the following activities:

1. Build your current and complete database of information in your professional portfolio. Chapter 4.

2. Build your current and complete standard vita. Chapter 5 and 6.

3. Build your current and complete standard resume. Chapter 7.

Now you are ready to face the challenge of various electronic resumes. Yes, resume is the most frequently used term in this emerging area, though the request for detailed information may take two to six pages to adequately produce.

New Rules

DO:

- Use a clear format.
- Use white paper.
- Use black ink.
- Use large font styles of ten points or larger.
- Use key words from job announcements.
- Use action verbs to describe accomplishments.

- Use headings as directed.
- Use laser, ink-jet, or letter-quality printing.

DO NOT:

- Use dark paper.
- Use fancy fonts such as script.
- Use a dot matrix printer.
- Use underlines.
- Use borders.
- Use graphic drawings, pictures, sketches, etc.

In short, keep it simple and straightforward, following the employers' instructions about style and format. Read and follow the specific job announcement very carefully for key word and specific skills, accomplishments, competencies etc. that are requested.

There are two recent books out that specialize in assistance for electronic resumes. For help in this area see:

Weddle, P. D. (1995). Electronic resumes for the new job market. Manassas, VA: Impact Publications.

For the new federal government resume see:

Troutman, K. K. (1995). The federal government guide book. Washington, D. C.: The Resume Place.

Create Your Own Home Page

Some people, especially those connected with higher education institutions or working in high tech parts of the country, are establishing their own home pages on the World Wide Web. This takes several key ingredients. (1)It takes a desire to advertise yourself and your resume in the most visible place in today's job market--the World Wide Web and (2) the personal or professional ability to create an attractive home page for your resume. The technical aspects of this go far beyond the scope of this book, but it represents an option for the applicant who want to take full advantage of the possibilities open to them.

Of course a person can send a cover letter and resume via e-mail. Remember the ground rules for an e-mail generated cover letter and resume are still governed by some of the suggestions in this book, plus the specific conditions set forth by the employer--such as the federal government and the specific details in any job opening announcement.

Chapter 10
Final Vita/Resume Check List

Understanding and following the principles of vita data collection and presentation can be a difficult process, unless care is taken to keep basic principles in mind. It is very easy--too easy--to slip in to careless habits unless care is taken to keep important points in mind.

Listed below, and for the last time, is a list of the ten points you should stress in developing your vita. These are also important in constructing the resume. Make sure you are using your qualifications in the most advantageous way to advance your career and professional life.

1.   **CONCEPTUALIZE**

- Be sure you know how you want to use your vita/resume.
- Be sure your vita/resume reflects your best interests.
- Be sure your vita/resume is written to inform readers who do not know you.

2.   **COMPLETE**

- Be sure your worksheets are complete.
- Be sure you have taken all key items from your worksheets.
- Be sure your vita/resume includes important data for your purposes.

3.   **CLEAR**

- Be sure a sound organization plan is followed.

- Be sure there are no confusing entries.
- Be sure it is readable.

4. CONCISE

- Be sure you vita/resume is not too long.
- Be sure your vita/resume is not padded.
- Be sure your vita/resume has no double entries.

5. CONSISTENT

- Be sure your vita/resume does not mix styles.
- Be sure your vita/resume has all sequences in the correct order.
- Be sure your vita/resume has an appearance of evenness.

6. CREATIVE

- Be willing to describe your skills and activities in full.
- Be willing to use short narrative statements to show special competencies.
- Be willing to cite papers, publications, or other creative works that you consider important.

7. CURRENT

- Be sure your vita/resume has no out-of-date entries.
- Be sure your vita/resume has a date.
- Be sure your vita/resume has recent important activities.

8. CONSIDERED

- Be sure your vita/resume is read by a professional colleague.
- Be sure your vita/resume is read by an employment official.
- Be sure your vita/resume is read by a good editor.

9.   **CORRECT**

- Be sure your vita/resume has the appearance of professional preparation.
- Be sure your vita/resume is error-free.
- Be sure your vita/resume is clearly duplicated.

10.   **COMPREHENSIVE**

- Be sure your cover letter gets a reader to want to see your vita/resume.
- Be sure your vita/resume sets a final check.
- Be sure everything is complete and correct.

Professional Portfolio Worksheets

An extra set of professional summary worksheets follows, as many readers may have used the first set in a training session and may now want a separate set to use to record their own data.

Use these worksheets as a basis for developing your own extensive data file--to be updated as significant events occur in your professional and personal file.

Professional Portfolio Worksheets

Name   **Date Prepared or Updated**

                                                 Social Security Number

Present Address:

_____

P. O. Box or Street

_____

City

_____

State   Zip Code

_____

Phone (Area Code)   Fax (Area Code)

_____

e-mail Address

Business Address

_____

Employed by (organization or institution)

_____

Job Title

_____

Phone (Area Code)   Fax (Area Code)

_____

P. O. Box or Street

_____

State   Zip Code

_____

e-mail Address

Permanent Address (if same as above leave blank)

_____

P. O. Box or Street

_____

City

_____

State   Zip Code

_____

Phone (Area Code)   Fax (Area Code)

_____

E-Mail Address

Other Personal Information

Birthplace   Birth Date
_____

Military Service Branch (if any)   Length of Service
_____

Title and Military Occupational Specialty Code
_____

Highest Rank Obtained   Awards
_____

Special Schools Completed
_____

Transferable Skills Obtained
_____

Educational Background (begin with most recent)

Degree   Date Graduated   Transcripts
_____

Major   Minor
_____

Institution
_____

Location   Zip Code
_____

Notes (Special honors or recognition)

Degree	Date Graduated	Transcripts

Major	Minor

Institution

Location	Zip Code

Notes (Special honors or recognition)

Degree	Date Graduated	Transcripts

Major	Minor

Institution

Location	Zip Code

Notes (Special honors or recognition)

Degree	Date Graduated	Transcripts

Major	Minor

Institution

Location	Zip Code

Notes (Special honors or recognition)

Other Training

(It is important to note yearly update and times as well as Continuing Education Units (CEU's), if appropriate. Include any independent study.

Employment Information

Work History (include full-time employment, internships, etc.--start with current position)

Position Title: Dates

Employer

Location   Zip Code

Supervisor   Title

Specific Responsibilities and Accomplishments

Position Title: Dates

Employer

Location   Zip Code

Supervisor   Title

Specific Responsibilities and Accomplishments

Position Title: _____ Dates _____

Employer _____

Location _____ Zip Code _____

Supervisor _____ Title _____

Specific Responsibilities and Accomplishments

_____

Position Title: _____ Dates _____

Employer _____

Location _____ Zip Code _____

Supervisor _____ Title _____

Specific Responsibilities and Accomplishments

_____

135

Position Title: **Dates**

Employer

Location   **Zip Code**

Supervisor   **Title**

Specific Responsibilities and Accomplishments

Position Title: **Dates**

Employer

Location   **Zip Code**

Supervisor   **Title**

Specific Responsibilities and Accomplishments

Position Title: _____ Dates _____

Employer _____

Location _____ Zip Code _____

Supervisor _____ Title _____

Specific Responsibilities and Accomplishments

_____

Other Employment (Include in this section part-time employment and jobs held during summer vacations, holidays, etc., and other employment not listed in the previous section. When doing this for the first time be complete to get your dates and records clear, then use only as it seems appropriate--if at all--in your vita.)

_____

_____

_____

_____

_____

Special Competencies (include teaching areas, artistic talents, organizational skills, supervisory skills, public speaking skills, sales ability, proposals funded, etc.)

_____

_____

_____

_____

Other Personal Data

_____

_____

_____

Certification or License Status with numbers and date issued

License	Authority	Expiration date

License	Authority	Expiration date

Computer Skills- Include knowledge of major applications such as desk-top publishing, spreadsheets, and word processing and/or database and programming skills.

_____

_____

_____

_____

Professional and Civic Activities

Memberships in Professional Associations (include both the name of the associations and offices you hold or have held with dates. Also any significant activities completed under your leadership.)

_____

_____

_____

_____

Professional and Civic Activities, cont.

_____

_____

_____

_____

_____

Religious Affiliation and Activities--including elected and appointed positions and dates.

_____

_____

_____

_____

Community Services Activities--including appointed and elected positions, with dates.

_____

_____

_____

_____

_____

_____

Leisure Activities--such as hobbies and volunteer involvement- notes skills, special responsibilities, elected or appointed leadership duties.

_____

_____

_____

Foreign languages--note written and spoken skill levels as well as major international travel or residence, note any special courses, training, and self-taught knowledge acquired.

_____

_____

_____

_____

Creative Professional Activities (include articles, books, reports, inventions, copyrights, or patents, paintings, poetry, music or plays written, exhibits displayed, etc.)

_____

_____

_____

_____

_____

Awards and Honors

_____

_____

_____

_____

_____

_____

_____

_____

_____

_____

Special Interests and Notes

References

Name
_____

Position
_____

Address
_____

Phone   Date confirmed
_____

Fax   Date confirmed
_____

Name
_____

Position
_____

Address
_____

Phone   Date confirmed
_____

Fax   Date confirmed
_____

Name

Position

Address

Phone   **Date confirmed**

Fax   **Date confirmed**

Name

Position

Address

Phone   **Date confirmed**

Fax   **Date confirmed**

Name _____

Position _____

Address _____

Phone _____ Date confirmed _____

Fax _____ Date confirmed _____

Name _____

Position _____

Address _____

Phone _____ Date confirmed _____

Fax _____ Date confirmed _____

Note: Select three to five from this listing for use in the actual vita, or if requested at an interview.